PRAISE FOR *THE*

"Brilliant, touching and at moments knee-slapping funny!"
—Navin Somani, Realtor

"Come along for one Daughter of God's journey through the movement of both her inner and outer world. There is laughter here and tears of release at knowing we are safe, loved and innocent, truly the Extension of Love Itself."
—Michael J. Miller, Poet

"In this wonderful book, the author shares her journey with her brothers and sisters who are consciously engaged on the path of awakening. *The Movement of Being* clearly portrays the differences between the right- and wrong-minded vantage points, and is most helpful for un-rutting false ego beliefs about ourselves. It provides clear insights on how to recognize Being, how to trust in Its Movement and how to experience the Movement of our own Being. Highly recommended for anyone on the path of awakening."
—Homer Lin, ACIM Taipei Taiwan

"More people need to know spiritual guidance is possible and to hear ways to receive guidance from those who do. Pauline has provided a personal and moving experience about her journey of awakening. *The Movement of Being* is filled with examples of how everyone can use each moment to step closer to their own shift in consciousness."
—Tim Alan Smith, author of *A Tiny Mad Idea*

The

Movement

of

Being

ALSO BY PAULINE EDWARD

Spirituality/A Course in Miracles

Choosing the Miracle

Leaving the Desert: Embracing the Simplicity of A Course in Miracles

Making Peace with God: The Journey of a Course in Miracles Student

Astrology and Numerology

Astrological Crosses: Exploring the Cardinal, Fixed, and Mutable Modes

The Power of Time: Understanding the Cycles of Your Life's Path

L'Hermès: Dictionnaire des correspondances symboliques, with Marc Bériault and Axel Harvey

Fiction

Wings of the Soul

The
Movement
of
Being

Pauline Edward

Desert Lily Publications
Montreal, Canada

Published by Desert Lily Publications, Montreal, Canada

Cover design: Pauline Edward; from the painting *Dance* by Marlise Witschi
Editorial consultation: Veronica Schami
V1.01

Library and Archives Canada Cataloguing in Publication
  Edward, Pauline, 1954-
  The movement of being / Pauline Edward.
  Includes bibliographical references.
  Issued in print and electronic formats.
  ISBN 978-0-9868909-3-2 (pbk.).--ISBN 978-0-9868909-5-6 (kindle).--
  ISBN 978-0-9868909-6-3 (smashwords)

      1. Course in Miracles. 2. Spiritual life. 3. Spiritual biography.
  4. Edward, Pauline, 1954-. I. Title.
  BP605.C68E396 2014   299'.93   C2014-902829-6
                                               C2014-902830-X

Contents

Author's Note

Although *A Course in Miracles* has become an important part of my work and my writing, I do not consider myself a *Course in Miracles* teacher or interpreter. As to who or what I am, I'm not quite sure any more. Let's just say that I'm rediscovering who I am as I allow myself to welcome miracles into my life.

Why do I write? I have asked myself that question a thousand times. Some thirty years ago, I set out to write one book, a novel. Although I had no intention of making writing a significant part of my life, here I am, with my eighth book. Why do I write? It just happens that writing has been helpful for my learning, perhaps an imprint from my youth, when it seemed that books were my only friends. However, because I am an author, it doesn't mean that I know everything or even much about anything at all! It just means that I am a writer.

Because I have written about my experience with the teaching of *A Course in Miracles*, it does not mean that I am a *Course in Miracles* expert or that I know more than you do; nor does it mean that the Course is the only path. We are alike, you and I, both children of God, seeking to awaken to the wholeness of our Being as God created us. It just so happens that the beauty, the simplicity, the directness of the message of *A Course in Miracles* appeals to me, perhaps as it does to you. Why do I write? I write because I enjoy it, which is reason enough.

For those who are familiar with my last book, *Choosing the Miracle*, you are aware that I accepted Jesus as my teacher and friend. Jesus invites us all to join and engage in conversation with him, and at a time when I was in great need of help, I dared to take him up on his offer. This friendship involves conversations, mostly with me asking for help and then listening for answers. While I was first trying to get a better understanding of how to integrate the teaching of *A Course in Miracles* in my life, many of my questions required lengthy answers. I recorded most of these answers, then transcribed them, followed by minor editing for readability. In the pages that follow, I have included many of the answers that I received from Jesus, my friend, as I refer to him throughout the book; these messages have been offset from the main narration with quotation marks. Some answers follow specific questions, while other sections are more in the form of teaching and learning aids. The latter were gathered over a period of several months and then grouped by topic.

Because minds are joined, messages received from our guides, from Jesus or from the Father reflect that which already exists in our own Right Mind, the truth. It has occurred to me, as it may to you, that the guidance I received might have come from my own Right Mind. If that was the case, then I am grateful for the joining, for it has greatly facilitated my learning. To focus on the source of the message, to compare, analyze or look for differences in teachings would be to play into the ego's game. One thing is certain, the ego would not encourage anyone to join with an awakened brother, much less seek to be in the Presence of God. The truth is easy to recognize; it is kind, loving and suits the needs of the moment.

For those readers who are unfamiliar with Jesus or for those who may be uncomfortable with the idea of having conversations with Jesus, simply imagine a dialogue with an enlightened older brother, a friend, someone who has your best interests at heart or simply the wise voice from within. The understated presentation of my dialogue with guidance in this book is deliberate and serves to avoid unduly placing too much importance on this relationship. The last thing we need is one more special individual with whom to engage in one more special relationship. Specialness is what got us into trouble in the first place.

It will soon become clear that the Jesus of *A Course in Miracles* is not the Jesus portrayed by our religions. The Jesus of the Course is smart as a whip, always loving and very down-to-earth. He also presents himself as an equal; he is, after all, our brother. The only difference is that he is awake and we are not. His sole purpose is to help us awaken, as is the case with all our awakened brothers and sisters who are waiting for us to reach out and ask for help.

Some people are uncomfortable, as I once was, with references to God, the Father. If this poses a problem, simply replace the word "God" with "Supreme Being," "Mother," "Source," "the All," "Love," "Eternal Life Principle," "Universe," "Infinite Life Principle" or whatever term connotes a loving, infinite presence. I have referred to Reality as the Kingdom of Heaven, or Home, that place where awakening leads us. The term "ego" refers to the part of our minds that identifies with the small, made-up, separated self that is asleep. "Awakening" and "enlightenment" refer to the complete release from the dream state and the rejoining with our Source. Note that it is not necessary to have studied *A Course in Miracles* to read this book; references to the Course are minimal.

Although words like "Heaven," "God" and "Christ" are used, they probably have more in common with Advaita Vedanta than Christianity. While we still have a need for words, their form does not have to get in the way of their meaning. When it comes to expressing a Soul's journey, words become inadequate. Only the heart can fully appreciate meaning.

Most of the personal stories related in this work fall in the category of minor incidences, maybe trivial for some readers. In a way, the lack of extreme circumstances may actually act as an impediment to the desire to wake up. In the absence of severe distress or "hitting the bottom of the barrel," what motivation is there to consider that there might be something else, something far better than what is being experienced? When life is good, why rock the boat! While my life has been good, there is no denying that, for as long as I can remember, I have felt an urge to reach beyond the limitations of physical perception and experience, and uncover the truth about Reality. It is this unnamed urge to have an experience of the more that is here that has fuelled my quest for awakening; it is this quest that I share in my writings.

Acknowledgments

Thank you, Raj/Jesus, for answering our call for help. There are not enough words in the universe to convey my gratitude for your love and especially your patience with your motley charge. Thank you, thank you, thank you.

Thank you, Paul and Susan Tuttle, and everyone at the Northwest Foundation for *A Course in Miracles,* for your courage and devotion to helping us bumbling brothers and sisters in our awakening.

I would also like to say "thank God," but that would sound cliché and empty, yet I do thank God, our Father, every day for never having abandoned us, no matter how far we seem to have strayed from our true Home. Thank You, Father, for placing on my path all that is necessary for awakening, but also for ensuring that my day to day needs are met.

Thank You for the wonderful friends You have sent to share the journey with me—Veronica, Pooran, Helena, Mike and so many more. Thank you, Marlise, for allowing yourself to live and reveal what is divine in you through your beautiful paintings. Thank you to the clients who ask those questions that require that I listen more closely to guidance and, in that listening, allow me to witness the beauty and awesomeness of their divine essence.

Thank you, thank you, thank you.

Chapter 1

A Friend on the Journey

Do you want a friend? Raj, *Graduation*

Stumbling into Grace

It had been nearly a decade since I plunged headfirst into the study of *A Course in Miracles*. Without a moment of hesitation, I claimed it as my pathway to salvation, instantly recognizing it as the incredible bridge to awakening that it is. There would be no stopping me; nothing in Heaven or earth could have lured me away from my divine pursuit. Finally, I had found what I had sought all my life—the truth, plain and simple. Here was the teaching that could and, more importantly, would take me home.

Regardless of the fact that I believed it was likely going to take all of my remaining years, perhaps even more, to reach my lofty goal—far too long for someone so intent on getting home—I dove in with the same exuberance and dedication with which I had embraced each and every other important undertaking of my life. Nor did it matter that I found the book incredibly difficult to read, let alone even begin to comprehend. I was determined to overcome my temporary learning disability, learn this Course and, above all, get it right. There was no doubt in my mind. This was my ticket home, I thought with great enthusiasm and self-satisfaction. Finally, I was going home; there was nothing I wanted more. I was going to leave this body, leave this world and all of its ever-increasing complexities and I was going home! In all sincerity, I thought there was actually somewhere else beyond this world to aim for, some great, peaceful, uncomplicated place, and that was where I was headed. I was going home!

As the full meaning of the message of the Course began to sink in, a radical new realization hit me with a force sufficient to cause the disintegration of all of my neat, logical, reassuring beliefs. The truth is that there really is no place else to go. If the world as I see it is an illusion, then in its place there must be Reality. This means that I am, we are and always have been, right in the middle of the Kingdom of Heaven. In one staggering flash of revelation, my best-laid plan for an imminent return to a home that was right here all along collapsed.

"Stop saying that you want to go home," my dear friend, channeller Lisa LaJoie, had admonished me on more than one occasion. Each time had left me feeling more perplexed than the last. Nevertheless, I wanted to wake up; more precisely, I wanted to leave this world and this body. It was a desire I had clung to ever since I could remember. Did this mean that all the work I had done with the Course was for naught? I had worked so hard to develop a clear, systematic, logical understanding of the metaphysics of *A Course in Miracles* and, suddenly, it dawned on me that my hard-earned learning might have been seriously flawed.

When my study of the Course came to a crashing halt and my precious plan for salvation fell apart, two important events occurred. The first, probably the most significant eye-opener of my life—or perhaps even of many lifetimes—was that I don't know shit! Well, let's qualify that a bit: of myself, as a separate, independent-thinking individual, I don't know shit. This was a big realization, a down-on-my-knees humbling realization, considering that it came after half a century of studying, pondering, analyzing, questioning and thinking, not to mention teaching, counselling and writing several books. Yet, as much as this glaring flash of insight might have been insulting to my cherished intelligence, instead it brought a profound sense of relief. Actually, it also brought a certain perverse sense of joy. I no longer needed to study, ponder, analyze, question or learn. As for "thinking," well, that was another matter and would be dealt with soon enough.

This new awareness triggered the release of a long-held, deeply rooted belief—that knowledge, in and of itself, is important, that intellectual understanding is an integral part of awakening and, more importantly, that my understanding mattered. I was about to discover that there is really no need to understand everything or to know how everything works, nor why it works or does not work. Going home or awakening to the fullness of our Divine Being—or, in loftier language, enlightenment—does not require the learning of complex theories about existence or the development of any special skills. In fact, all past learning and conceptions must ultimately be abandoned to allow for a full experience of the Truth. All that is required is the willingness to consider the possibility that the Light lies within us and has actually never left us, and the willingness to trust in the unfolding that will occur once our attention has been turned in its direction.

The second significant event occurred when I finally accepted that I did not need to make the journey home alone; actually, I could use a little help. Okay, perhaps I could use a whole lot of help. Though at first somewhat disorienting, given my independent nature, this realization brought yet another profound and welcome sense of relief. There was no need to pursue this path alone. In fact, this journey was nearly impossible to undertake alone. I needed a friend; I wanted a friend. I needed a friend who was awake and who could and would steer me in the right direction whenever I veered off course, which occurred more frequently than I care to admit.

What might have been perceived as a fall from grace, this hitting the bottom of the barrel, turned out to be a stumbling into grace. These two seemingly simple yet important realizations set the stage for the next leg of the journey, and here the term "journey" is being used loosely, for there really is no journey. There is only the temporary delay we experience when we choose against the full acceptance of the truth of who and where we are in our state of unalterable divine wholeness. It is a delay we experience every moment we choose to continue our little experiment of separation from our Source. Abandoning independent thinking and asking for help ultimately led to the wonderful gifts of grace that would follow—the gifts that lie in waiting for the moment we relinquish control over who and what we are, thus allowing the full expression of our true Being as God created us.

Jesus and Me

If someone had told me that one day I would be carrying on conversations with Jesus, I would have thought the idea completely preposterous, perhaps even insane. Actually, during the first several years of working with *A Course in Miracles*, whenever I heard of anyone channelling Jesus, I would recoil with a narrow-minded, defensive, knee-jerk reaction. Why would Jesus channel through someone else when he had spent seven years channelling the Course through Helen Schucman? We have everything we need in the Course—make that the official version of the Course—the most special spiritual work in existence—ever. So why would he channel something more to someone else? What's more, Jesus was, well, he was Jesus, and Helen, who must have been much holier than you and me and most everyone else, had been chosen by Jesus, no less, to perform the very special holy task of scribing this very special holy book. Never mind that it didn't occur to me that a work that teaches that there is no hierarchy of illusions should also not have a hierarchy of teachers and students, this was a safe, separation-maintaining way of seeing that my fearful ego-identified self clung to dearly. More importantly, this reaction reflected the profound fear and desperation of the dwindling false self that was undergoing a systematic regimen of dismantling.

Nonetheless inquisitive and not fully accepting this fearful and limited appreciation for the help made available to us by our enlightened brother, I asked Lisa during a reading how it was that so many different people could be channelling Jesus. The answer was quick and to the point: "I am everywhere." Of course, he would be. He is awake and, furthermore, since all minds are joined, he is available to commune with anyone who asks for his help, including you and me.

Although I consider myself to be a relatively successful and independent do-it-yourselfer, I fortunately did come to accept that awakening was going to be a two-person job with me on the sleeping side and a helper on the awakened side. In spite of my cherished self-reliance, it was a relief to learn that I would not be alone as I walked forth into what appeared as foreign and, at times, frightening—even terrifying—territory. I would soon learn that where I was going was home, and so was not a foreign place at all. What I needed was a hand to hold while I dared to open myself up to the full possibilities of the Reality that awaited, ready to replace the limited experience served up by my sleeping ego-identified self.

I must admit that at first I did feel a slight twinge of uneasiness, even just considering the possibility that I might actually be having conversations with Jesus. It wasn't so much because of doubt in the possibility of communication, but more an issue of worthiness. Why would Jesus speak to *me*? What had I done to merit such special favour? However, this issue was quickly resolved when I reminded myself of a few basic facts. We are all expressions of the Mind of God: you, me, Jesus, your teenage daughter, your ex, your favourite political, religious or corporate punching bag, the one you consider your biggest forgiveness partner in this lifetime, the one you just can't quite seem to forgive for his indisputably unfair treatment of you. We are created from love: whole, undivided, all of us joined as God's eternal ongoing Expression. This means that no one is special, including Helen or even Jesus, and no one is less than special, including you and me and the one you just can't seem to forgive. Furthermore, Jesus makes it clear that we should consider him as our brother, for this is who he considers himself to be. As he tells us in Chapter 1 of the Course:

> Equals cannot be in awe of one another because awe implies inequality…. There is nothing about me that you cannot attain. I have nothing that does not come from God. The main difference between us as yet is that I have nothing else. This leaves me in a state of true holiness, which is only a potential in you. (ACIM, Ch.1)

If Jesus were better than we were, if he had something we did not have, if he were really the special chosen Son of God, we would be in serious trouble, for how could we ever hope to attain his level of awakening if we were missing some essential attribute? Hierarchies of brothers and sisters would imply specialness, differences and unfairness, which would imply judgment and selectiveness on the part of our Creator, which is impossible, for that which is born of the undivided Mind of God remains always whole and perfect, like that Mind. Since nothing exists outside the Mind of God, then inequality is simply not possible. To perceive separateness or differences requires that we make up our own definitions of what God has created; it is to imagine an alternative to Reality and so it is to make up an illusion.

To think that I could continue on my journey of awakening all by my separated, isolated, oh-so-independent and highly capable self without the support of an awakened brother would have constituted an act of insanity. Awakening is an act of joining and joining is an act of sanity. It leads to an awareness of the oneness of all of creation, to an experience of joining with what the Source, or God, is Being in the moment. It is not the result of assiduous training, self-study, personal development, wilfulness, individual effort or, more importantly, intellectual understanding. Since to awaken is to return to sanity—our natural, normal, whole state—it requires the abandonment of self-directed, independent action and thinking, including the desire to understand everything and even the desire to understand the process of awakening. If I wanted to awaken, which I did want, I would have to quit trying to do it on my own. I would have to reach out and take the hand that was offered. Furthermore, I would have to trust that I would be led out of the dream in a manner that was appropriate for the circumstances of my life, respectful of my fear of awakening and comfortable for me.

Do You Want a Friend?

Being of a thinking, analytical temperament, I was very familiar with mental chatter. The question now was, how would I know whose voice I was listening to when I engaged in my silent conversations? With whom was I carrying on my captivating mental dialogues? Most of the time, my mental real estate was preoccupied with the hustle and bustle of day-to-day concerns, a familiar chatter that clearly belonged to my self, the small, separated self that believed that it was possible to be, do and think independently of the Father.

Besides my customary mental chatter, I became aware of a clear, slow, gentle yet firm voice that I came to recognize as the voice of sanity. One way in which I was able to distinguish it from the voice of the small self is that, rather than it addressing what I perceived to be the problems and issues at hand, it instead pointed me to the true source of the problem. Common problem areas included guilt, fear, lack of trust, belief in my littleness, impatience, the desire to do things independently and fear of love, just to name a few. However, there was one catch to hearing this voice: I could not hear anything if I did not want to hear it, which, unfortunately, occurred more frequently than I would have liked.

I suppose I could have referred to this quiet, steady, sane voice as the voice of my "imaginary" Jesus, but, being that there was already enough imaginary stuff in my dream of imaginary separation, I liked to think of my joining with my wise older brother as being among the few real experiences worthy of my attention. It is the one joining that gave me the strength and the courage to continue on this journey, the one joining to which I needed to pay more attention.

It did occur to me that perhaps this was all just my wild imagination at work—just me, talking to myself. At the same time, I was also aware that there remained a part of me that liked being separate, a part of me that feared the complete joining that awakening promises. The small voice of the ego-identified self was very different from the sane voice that guided me gently forward. The small voice was insane, anxious, fearful, angry, confused, indecisive, defensive, impatient, judgmental and self-righteous. It claimed that there was something wrong, that something needed fixing and it pointed to my, or someone else's, guilt. It looked outside my mind for the cause of troubles in my life. The small voice of the ego stirred up fear and doubt, built a case for my vulnerability and chipped away at feelings of deep peace. It raised suspicion in the face of expressions of love, and it would have liked to convince me that I was a victim of forces beyond my control. This voice was easy to recognize, and I no longer cared to pay attention to it.

The sane voice was quite different and could be heard when I was peaceful and quiet, during meditation, in the middle of the night, early in the morning upon waking or while out for my daily walks. In fact, daily walks became like a form of moving meditation during which I could focus on being quiet and pay attention to what God was expressing in whomever or whatever I encountered, no matter what was going on. Walking meditations became more conducive to peaceful connection with guidance than sitting meditations because I was not confronted with the distractions of making my body comfortable, nor could I fall asleep, a favourite display of resistance to the practice of being in the Presence of God. In the end, it was during these walking meditations that I would experience some of my most profound moments of revelation. But I digress; more on this later.

One day, overcome by an onslaught of distracting thoughts that had invaded my mind like a room full of toddlers all at once clamouring for my attention, I asked Jesus how I could tell which voice I was hearing. The quick and direct answer was, "How many voices do you think there are?" Okay. He does have a way of shutting down my senseless, complicated, analytical questioning. It looked as though he was going to keep his word, something he had promised a while back, "I will make it simple for you." Of course, there is only one true voice; the false voice is easy to recognize, and needs only be ignored. The voice for truth comes from a place of peace, while the ego seeks to destroy peace. That was indeed simple enough, and being tired of complications, I very much appreciated the simplicity of truth.

Despite having almost without question accepted the practice of being and conversing with Jesus, I did, on occasion—okay, make that frequently—fall prey to doubt. However, each time the doubt was cleared away with appropriate guidance. I would simply remind myself, since I didn't know shit, what did I have to lose?

With persistence and first-hand experience, it became evident that the guidance I received when I was in that quiet, receptive state of mind must be valid because it offered a clearly enlightened perspective on the issue at hand, something the ego would not provide. This guidance was clear, straightforward, intelligent and consistent; it always contributed to the resolution of the situation or problem and left me feeling comforted and supported. It never added to my fears, doubts or uncertainty—as was the case when I relied on the ego—and it addressed the real issue. This guidance was kind, patient and always appropriate, but, most of all, it was always loving.

There is no doubt that I needed a friend. I needed someone with whom I could share my fears, my doubts and my uncertainties without being judged for my numerous failings. I needed someone with whom I could check to see if I was moving in the right direction and, when I was stuck, to see how I could get myself unstuck. When I accepted to take the hand of Jesus on this journey, I gave myself the greatest gift of all, the gift of a true friend. This gift of love, support and gentle guidance has been offered to every one of us. The gift has been made; it requires only that we accept it. Besides, a gift remains incomplete until it is accepted, and so to accept this gift is an act of wholeness, it is an act of love.

I really like having Jesus as my friend on the journey. He laughs with me, sometimes, he even laughs at me; he lets me cry and he never judges me. No matter what I am experiencing or how I am feeling, I know that he just loves me. No matter the tone of his guidance, which can sometimes be quite direct, he loves me. Even when I get upset with him, impatient with myself and angry because the journey is so difficult, he still loves me.

"Historically speaking, I am the one who was known as Jesus.... Now I am present with and available to every single one of you, everyone at every moment. And so it is my intent in being with groups of people like this to make this fact known, and by Paul's presence and demeanor, also convey the fact that my being available doesn't require of anyone any special talent, because Paul is about as regular as anyone else on this planet and has no "special" talent in order to hear me.

"For those of you who are students of *A Course in Miracles*, I will take this opportunity to point out that my time spent with Helen Schucman was also not a special instance. And although there have been some expressions of the [...] idea that everyone else can't expect the same sort of relationship with me or with guidance that she experienced, [this] is untrue. It is an attempt to elevate her, and to elevate the Course into a false position of religious respect, whether it is stated that way or not." (Raj/Jesus communing with Paul Tuttle of the Northwest Foundation for *A Course in Miracles*, 1994, Princeville, HI)

In *Graduation*, Raj gives Paul the following instructions: "I want you to make a sticker and put it on the face of your computer monitor. The words on it are to say, 'Do you want a friend?'"

I wrote those words on a yellow Post-it note and placed it on my monitor. Yes, I thought, I do want a friend.

Do *you* want a friend?

Chapter 2

Connecting with Guidance

I will step back and let Him lead the way. (ACIM.W.155)

Is Guidance for You?

Whether you are a student of *A Course in Miracles* or another spiritual teaching, or perhaps not a student of any spiritual teaching, you can connect with guidance and enjoy the invaluable benefits that joining brings. Actually, the lack of any prior training or preconceived ideas about the subject may mean fewer obstacles to your enjoyment of what is essentially a simple practice. The less you try to understand how it works and how well it is working for you, the easier it will be. The reason it is so simple is that, being an act of joining, connecting with guidance is natural. It does not require exceptional gifts or abilities, the practice of complicated rituals or special training. It requires only a desire to join and a little perseverance —okay, maybe a lot of perseverance. If you have reached a point in your life where you have concluded that you just cannot do it alone any more, then you are already almost there.

With an open mind and the willingness to consider that perhaps guidance might be there for the asking, your experience will be greatly facilitated. It may be helpful to assume that, if you have asked for guidance, your request has been heard. If the nature of our Source is love, a call for help can only be responded to with love. If you are having difficulty with the idea of speaking with your guide, think about how you have been faring as a separate, isolated entity, most likely conversing or debating with the ego, who, as we know, does not have your best interests in mind. Would you be willing to consider, just for a moment, that perhaps there might be a better partner with whom to share the journey? Besides, what do you have to lose? What's more, there is no need to tell anyone that you are talking with the Holy Spirit or your guide or Jesus or God or the Buddha, and so you need not worry about what people will say or think. Connecting with guidance is an inside job and remains always between you and your guide.

Another point worth considering is that you have already been guided in your life; everyone has been guided. Simply look back at those times when you felt completely lost, without hope and alone, and something or someone came along and gave perhaps the smallest of nudges that allowed you to move to a better place. Anything that helps us regain equilibrium or obtain healing is certainly not from the ego. Wholeness, resolution, healing, joy and peace are of the nature of our Source. No matter how seemingly insignificant, everyone has received help when it was most needed.

The following is a straightforward and effective four-step approach for connecting with guidance, as taught by Paul Tuttle and Raj of the Northwest Foundation for *A Course in Miracles*. Simply bring to it the curiosity of a child, free of doubts and preconceived ideas. Hold no expectation other than to be heard. Know that if you have asked for help, you have been heard, for that is the nature of love. Since love is our birthright, it remains with us always.

First, be still. Employ whatever means are at your disposal to be quiet, to cease all meaningless mental activity and to set aside all mundane concerns. The daily practice of meditation is a helpful method for training the mind to be quiet and is an effective way to prepare for connecting with guidance. Sit in a comfortable chair, in any position that allows for the absence of distractions, in a quiet room, perhaps with a "Do Not Disturb" sign on the door—in a hot bath, in the garden or, if all else fails, in your car, in the quiet of your garage. Lying down in bed is probably not as effective as an upright position because the greater likelihood of falling asleep.

Next, state clearly and simply your desire to be in communication with your guide, the Holy Spirit, Jesus, your guardian angel, a favourite saint or with whatever form of guidance feels right for you at the moment. Do not repeat your request like a mantra or an affirmation; rather, express it as a clear statement of your sincere intention to establish this connection. Repetition implies lack of trust in your hearing ability, as well as lack of hearing ability on the part of your guide. Even if you doubt that you will be heard, just say it as if you mean it and know that you have been heard. It is impossible that love would deny a call for help.

Then, be still and listen for a response until you sense a connection, or for as long as is comfortable. At first, answers may not come right away. When the urge to quit arises, give it a couple more minutes. This strengthens your resolve to establish a relationship and obtain an answer. After that, if nothing comes to you, then simply go about your normal business. Know that an answer is forthcoming, perhaps at a more appropriate moment, in a manner that will be easiest for you to grasp.

Finally, expect a response. Raj makes it clear that this is an important step: it establishes that your intent is sincere, it opens the door for receiving help and it begins to foster trust, an essential component to any deep and worthwhile relationship. To simply ask a question and not expect an answer would be like casting a fishing line with no expectation of catching anything. Also, to expect a response is a clear statement of your sense of worthiness: you deserve an answer for the simple reason that you, as a child of God, have asked for help. There are no prerequisites and no conditions to be met before guidance can be received. All that is needed is the willingness to ask, be quiet, listen and expect an answer.

Soon after having connected, an answer may come in a form that is easy to recognize, such as a flash of insight, an inspired vision, unquestionable clarity, a strong knowing or a simple sense, or a feeling of what is right. It may also come later, perhaps even when least expected: in a dream, in the words of a song or even on a billboard along the road. With practice, guidance takes the form of a conversation between you and your guide, with questions being asked and answers being given. You may find it helpful to have a pen and paper handy to write what comes to you from guidance.

For the first several months, I tended to receive guidance either in the middle of the night or just upon waking in the morning. Not overly fond of turning on the lights and writing notes while half asleep, I purchased a small digital recorder that has since found a place by my side day and night. Guidance comes at those times when the mind is least distracted by the affairs of the day, therefore less guarded and more receptive. Oddly, I have also received snippets of guidance while driving the car. It appears that being focused on the mechanics of driving and paying attention to road signals enhances the ability to hear guidance. Of course, this occurs in calm driving conditions, not under the stress of navigating road construction and heavy traffic. Another fruitful time for connecting with guidance is during daily walks, again a time when the mind is not as preoccupied with the distractions of work. Personal experiences with this practice are illustrated in a later chapter.

One of the great benefits of recording the messages received from guidance is that, when reviewed later, it becomes clear that the information could not have come from the ego. Many times while transcribing a recorded message, I scratch my head and wonder how I could possibly have forgotten the words but, more importantly, how incredibly insightful and spot-on they were. In a process that serves to undo the ego, it will attempt to bury any little bit of insight that poses a threat to its existence; failure to remember is one of its favourite tools. Communing with guidance is not an activity that will be willingly supported by the ego, whose basis for existence is the practice of separation.

Chances are that an answer might not be heard on the first try or even for the first couple of weeks, sometimes longer. Know that if you have asked for help, you have been heard and guidance is present. No one is ever refused support; no one is left to make the journey home alone. Patient persistence is the key to establishing the connection. Just as you would not turn away a toddler tugging at your pant leg requesting your attention, you will not be refused the support and guidance that you seek.

Why Is Connecting with Guidance Important?

Connecting with guidance is essential to awakening because it is an act of joining. Joining is the exact opposite of separation, which is an act that can only lead to an illusory state, a state of sleep. In Biblical terms, joining reverses the fall of man; it nullifies the idea that it is preferable to be separate from the Father. In *Course in Miracles* terms, it reverses the thought of separation. In order for separation and existence outside of perfect Oneness to appear to be real, one must find another person who supports the idea. Though a simple foolish idea, separation is seemingly made real when two join in agreement to pretend that it is possible.

In order to awaken, it is essential to join with someone who does not support the idea of separation. There must be a willingness to consider that perhaps separation is not our true condition, that perhaps there is something better. There must be a willingness to consider that the alternative, or awakening to the full experience of Being, might be worthy of our attention. Connecting with guidance or, in *Course in Miracles* terms, establishing a holy relationship, is important because it is a joining that corrects an act of joining that has an error as an outcome, that is, the belief in separation.

Working with Guidance

Your relationship with your guide will be unique to you and may be completely unlike your friend's or your partner's relationship with their guide. It is likely to be in accordance with your personality style, character and education, thus facilitating interaction and understanding. Because the style of language may resemble your own, this should not be taken as an indication that imagination is at work and you must, therefore, be hearing your own voice. Imagination is the stuff of the ego and is easy to recognize. What is received from guidance will be practical, within the boundaries of your current level of understanding and it will be geared to address the situation at hand in the most appropriate and efficient manner. This means that the same question posed at a later date might lead to a different answer, especially if your level of understanding has shifted. For this reason, it is best not to make a formula or set of hard and fast rules about how guidance should be received, or about the nature of information received through guidance.

By spending quiet time connecting with your guide or the Holy Spirit daily, you will become familiar with the form of communication that works best for you. Guidance is likely to come in a form that you can understand; it will not come in a foreign language or in a form that is beyond your level of comprehension. Guidance comes when you are in a peaceful, receptive frame of mind. Very importantly, guidance comes when you have relinquished personal expectations and desires, as well as the need to control and, naturally, the belief that you know what is best for all concerned. This means that you have decided and accepted to yield completely into the truth, no matter the outcome.

Guidance is also likely to meet your need in a practical way, and will be simple and readily applicable should there be a need for action on your part. If you think that you have been guided to jump through hoops, quit your day job, pack a tent and move to the South Pole or engage in what appears foolish and impractical, you can bet your blue book that you have been guided by the ego. Guidance can take many forms: a feeling that you are to go in a certain direction, a phrase in a book or something that someone says during a chance meeting. Clarification can be triggered in countless ways; all that is needed is a welcoming openness on our part.

Connecting with guidance can be most helpful for gaining insights on the journey to awakening, but it is also very beneficial for dealing with the business of everyday life. It would be foolish to limit this practice to spiritual applications alone, since the journey of awakening is traced right through the centre of our everyday existence, through our essential Being. While helpful for finding practical solutions, the practice of asking for guidance with ordinary daily situations is also a fun way to strengthen our relationship with our guide while building confidence in the process.

A further benefit of joining with guidance for everyday matters is that it makes it easier to join when in crisis, when noise and confusion block the ability to hear. Having developed a relationship with guidance, you will be familiar with how it feels to be joined with a sane mind. It will then be easier to release the chaotic and unsettling insanity that has temporarily taken over, and yield to the calm, peaceful support of guidance.

But, Am I Really Hearing Guidance?

How do you know for sure that you are hearing the voice of your guide, the Holy Spirit or Jesus, and not the voice of the ego? In truth, you may not know for sure, at least not at first. However, with practice, you will come to have a clear sense of which voice you are hearing. As everyone's relationship with their guide is unique, it may not be a good idea to compare notes with a friend, at least until you have developed a certain level of trust in your relationship with your own guide.

There are many telltale signs that can help sort out the voice for Truth from the ego's cunning chatter, the first being peace. The ego's invitations—for that is all they can ever be—are enticing, exciting and usually filled with some form of emotional charge, such as anticipation, a sense of righteousness, confusion, fear, doubt, anxiety, guilt, a promise of a payoff, a sense of justice or vindication. A message from your guide will come from a place of peace, will be clear and will be appropriate for your needs at the time. It may even be so practical as to appear boring, but that would only mean that you are listening with the ego. The ego does not really like boring; it prefers drama.

Building a Relationship with Guidance

The best place to start is with simple yes or no questions. Should I go to the store today? Is there mail in the mailbox? Will the item I want to purchase be on sale? Should I take this lane to avoid traffic? Should I make a right turn? Is this the best time to call my daughter? Ask, be quiet and listen. The practice of asking simple questions and listening for answers will increase your confidence in your ability to join. Spiritual practice is not just for when you are sitting in your meditation room or visiting an ashram; it is for when you are driving the car, washing the dishes, waiting for a flight, mowing the lawn, sending the kids off to school, fixing a leaky faucet or attending a business meeting.

At times, you may be guided by a feeling rather than by words. Right action or the appropriate response to a situation usually feels right. This right feeling is peaceful, quiet and usually leads to a simple, uncomplicated resolution to your quandary. Sometimes this feeling guides you to take no action at all. Many times, the absence of activity is the right response to a situation. Always, guidance comes from the quiet place within, or if it appears to come from outside, it is acknowledged as being right from that quiet place within.

In time, you will come to appreciate that your relationship with guidance is for every day, all day and every minute of the day. It isn't just for when a serious problem, question or need arises. Joining is essential to being in the waking state full-time. As such, joining with guidance is a full-time occupation that is the answer to the full-time preoccupation with the illusion of separation from wholeness.

What if you don't understand the guidance you have received? First, let it sit for a while. Then, ask your guide for further clarification. Also, do not be afraid to question or disagree with your guide. Your guide is there to meet you where you are, at your current level of understanding. This is a two-way relationship—a partnership. The more completely you engage in this interaction, the more beneficial the relationship will be. Remember that guidance is important, because it is a first-hand experience of joining; it is a way of breaking the isolation that is at the core of most of our problems as separated, sleeping individuals. The practice of regularly joining with guidance begins to break down the habit of independent thinking and action. It weakens the shell of isolation that was built to differentiate and protect the separated self.

Chances are, at least in the beginning, that on more than one occasion you will have heard incorrectly. It is best not to analyze the results of joining with guidance. Whether or not you heard right is not important. What is important is that you have joined. It is not in the ego's best interests for you to succeed or to hear correctly. It will want to prove that joining does not work and that you cannot do it properly. Don't even bother going down that road. If you seek out and analyze all the times that you heard incorrectly, you will be proving the ego's point. It is important to remember that it is not in the ego's best interests that you join. Therefore, simply ignore the ego's objections, no matter how clever or how logical they seem. Besides, how well has listening to the ego ever worked out?

Sometimes, connecting with guidance is just a matter of joining. There was a period of several weeks when, while I was out for my daily walks, recorder in my pocket, no significant guidance came. On those walks, I simply joined and walked in silent presence. One day, curious about the conspicuous absence of messages I asked my walking companion if I was doing something wrong. "Sometimes, simple communion, joining in silence is sufficient. You don't have to talk all the time; you don't have to ask questions all the time. Simply practise being with the more that is there." Feeling reassured, I knew that as I needed more input, it would be made available to me.

Another way to distinguish guidance from ego suggestions is that guidance will honour the integrity of you. It is not there to make others happy or to fulfill the ego agendas of others. It is not there to hurt or dishonour another, nor is it provided to make you feel superior, vindicated or righteous. That is the ego's function. Guidance is kind, loving and respectful of all concerned and it leads to a peaceful, loving and appropriate response, whether or not we understand its full meaning at the time it is received. Clarification usually comes once personal, or ego, investment has been withdrawn from the outcome.

As I was working on a section of this book, doubts about the guidance I had been receiving arose again. I had questions and I was receiving answers, but were they valid? I asked for help and was shown clearly that, since the nature of reality is wholeness, then on the edge of any question there must also reside the answer. To ask a question is to bring forth an answer. Since there are only two possible sources of answers and only one of these is true, it becomes a matter of simple discernment to distinguish between what comes from truth and what comes from falsity. Since each one of us shares the same Source of wholeness and truth, each one of us has the ability to discern between the two. The important thing is to remember to engage in an active dialogue with guidance. In your heart, you will know the truth.

> A healed mind does not plan. It carries out the plans that it receives through listening to wisdom that is not its own. It waits until it has been taught what should be done, and then proceeds to do it. It does not depend upon itself for anything except its adequacy to fulfill the plans assigned to it. It is secure in certainty that obstacles can not impede its progress to accomplishment of any goal that serves the greater plan established for the good of everyone. (ACIM.W.135)

Practical Guidance

While working on this chapter, I experienced an amusing example of guidance. I'm generally not a fan of shopping, much less shopping for clothes, but I had a mixed bag of errands on my to-do list, so I bundled them together and set aside a morning to get them done. At the top of the list was the purchase of an extended warranty for one of my new appliances; next, in desperate need of sweaters for the cooler months, a trip to Walmart; and, finally, a quick stop at the stationery store. It was mid-October—time to buy my agenda for the coming year. I still use a letter-sized hardcover agenda, an increasingly rare commodity in the age of digital devices, with availability limited to a few weeks in October and November. This was an important item on the list.

As I put the car in gear and rolled out of the driveway, I mulled over the Workbook lesson I had read earlier that morning. I was to practise looking with the eyes of Christ and hearing with His ears. By the time I reached the main street a short kilometre away, I was well engaged in the practice of looking with new eyes and hearing with new ears. Merging into mid-morning traffic, I joined with my brothers and sisters, appreciating the flow of life, sensing what God was Being in the world around me that sunny autumn day.

Usually, I plan my outings so that they are cost- and time-efficient, with the route mapped out to avoid traffic and unnecessary detours. It's just one of those quirks of my predominantly linear-thinking brain. In that quiet frame of mind I had slipped into, before I realized where I was going, I had steered the car into the far left lane; it would seem that a slight detour to the stationery store was in order. Okay, I thought, and mentally reshuffled my list to move the agenda to the top.

The store had undergone a light makeover since my last visit, and so I had to scour the aisles for a couple of minutes before finding the object of my search. There it was, the only agenda remaining on the shelf. Huh, I thought, glad not to have argued with the gentle impulse to veer away from my carefully planned, orderly itinerary.

The business with the extended warranty took much longer than expected, and so when I had the hunch to check out the Zellers next door instead of following my mapped-out route to the Walmart a few kilometres away, I decided to pay attention. Since I had been practising connecting with guidance with simple things, I was not surprised to find over half a dozen tables stacked with exactly what I was looking for, with a very nice discount to boot. Clearly, the practice of being still while remaining open to inspiration has its benefits.

> Brother, we find that stillness now. The way is open. Now we follow it in peace together. You have reached your hand to me, and I will never leave you. We are one, and it is but this oneness that we seek, as we accomplish these few final steps which end a journey that was not begun. (ACIM.W.225)

Tips for Working with Guidance

- Don't think about it or wonder if the whole thing might not be a little bit over the top or too esoteric for you; just do it!

- Persist. You are not likely to be successful on the first try, especially if you are new to meditation and connecting with guidance.

- It's never about the problem or the question; it's about joining.

- Avoid the temptation to analyze or question the validity of the information you receive. Instead, see how it feels.

- Become familiar with the ego's language and proclivities. It will be easier to differentiate its voice from that of your guide.

- The voice for truth always comes from peace.

- The ego's advice will not likely lead to peace. It may lead to temporary joy, self-satisfaction or exhilaration, but that is not peace.

- Your guide is your equal, your friend; don't be afraid to express yourself as you would with a dear friend.

- Expect simple, practical solutions and insights.

- Ask your question and then leave it alone. The answer may come when you least expect it, very likely when you are quiet, unconcerned and peaceful.

- Practise with simple questions.

- The practice of joining with guidance gradually breaks the habit of self-protection and isolation.

- Don't be afraid to question the guidance you receive and ask for further clarification when it appears unclear.

- Your guide's function is to be of assistance; it is therefore most wise to seek out and welcome that assistance.

- The more diligent you are in developing a quiet mind, the easier it will be to listen for guidance.

- It's never about the answer or the outcome; it's about joining.

  Joining greatly speeds up awakening.

  Accept the gift of guidance, for in your acceptance the joining has been made complete.

Chapter 3

A Shift in Perspective

God is my life. I have no life but His.

I was mistaken when I thought I lived apart from God, a separate entity that moved in isolation, unattached, and housed within a body. Now I know my life is God's, I have no other home, and I do not exist apart from Him. He has no Thoughts that are not part of me, and I have none but those which are of Him. (ACIM.W.223)

Hope for the Homeless

While my portrayal of the message of *A Course in Miracles* as expressed in *Leaving the Desert* may have been logical, perhaps even elegant, given my lack of actual experience of the teaching in my life, it was lacking some key elements. From my limited perspective, there appeared to be nothing to replace the illusion, nothing to stimulate sufficient curiosity to want to go beyond the illusion; there was, in fact, no hopeful outcome to awakening. There appeared to be no real reason for awakening from the dream. Instead, there was only a sense of an impending ending, although there was a certain appeal to the idea of seeing an end to the struggle for survival in a body trapped in a world with death as its unavoidable outcome. Awakening meant the end of separation and the cherished experience of autonomy and independence; more importantly, it meant the end of everything I knew of as myself. It sounded like it would mean the end of me. So, why should I pursue this path of awakening?

Maybe my home in this world was illusory, but it was an illusion with which I was familiar and, admittedly, quite comfortable. The only hope this journey of awakening offered was a promise of the end of suffering; but then life was not always about suffering— far from it— so that thought alone did not provide sustainable incentive. There had to be more. There had to be another level of motivation, something far greater than just the idea that everything would end, that pain would disappear and that the burden of life in a body and the need to deal with a complicated world of illusions would cease.

Barring a clear idea of what lay beyond the illusion, the only thing I could do was trust. I trusted my teacher implicitly. Jesus would not have given us this huge, complicated blue book and then spent hundreds of hours giving workshops with Paul Tuttle only to get us to the point of becoming nobody, with nothing to do, in a vast, unified and undefined nowhere. Clearly, I had misunderstood some of the teachings of the Course; corrections to my learning were in order. There was only one thing to do. I forgave myself for being such a slow learner, and I loved myself enough to keep plodding along.

Although for the most part I had accepted that I would not understand my way into the Kingdom of Heaven, I nevertheless had a few questions—make that many questions! Giving up the deeply engrained habit of thinking and analyzing—along with an unshakeable addiction to understanding—was going to take a bit of time, and I had the most patient teacher in the entire universe. So, why had Jesus said that the Course does not aim at teaching the meaning of love and that this was beyond what can be taught? How then were we supposed to attain this elusive love? Where was this love? What exactly was beyond the Course? At the very end of the book, he tells us that this Course is a beginning. What came after this new beginning? Another journey? The last thing I wanted was to engage in another pursuit; this quest had to end one day, hopefully sooner rather than later.

Then there were the cryptic early Workbook lessons in the Course, the ones I had glossed over the first time I read the book, judging them less relevant than the rest. *Nothing I see means anything. I have given everything I see the meaning that it has for me. These thoughts do not mean anything.* What was the true meaning of these lessons? These lessons must have some meaning or else Jesus would not have included them. Actually, what was the meaning of meaning? What was the meaning of anything!

I had spent considerable time and effort studying the Course and now I would have to learn something else. Somehow, this thought wasn't very appealing. If there was something else to be learned, what was it? The Course asks us to seek only the experience and not let theology delay us. I would have to start over and examine with fresh eyes what the Course was actually teaching. What was it really asking of us?

Intellectual understanding had gotten me to the point where I realized that there was something more to be experienced over and above intellectual understanding. In fact, intellectual understanding, no matter how personally gratifying it was, would have to be abandoned in favour of an actual experience of the truth. To cling to intellectual understanding was like an artist clinging to technique alone; no matter how excellent the technique, it alone would not make of him a true artist. He would eventually have to trust in something greater that would seek expression from within his Soul.

Though I was confused about what I knew and what I didn't know, I was very clear on one thing: I did not want to study any more theory, psychology, metaphysics, theology, spirituality or religion. I just wanted enough understanding to point me in the right direction, wherever that might be. However, I was curious. It was my nature, and I simply couldn't help myself. The Course teaches that there is a different way of seeing. This meant that there was something to be seen beyond or other than what I saw. There was something *more* to be experienced, and this raised more questions.

What was there to be experienced beyond the limits of current perception? What would replace the old way of seeing and thinking? If I was going to wake up and leave the illusion anyway, why should I work at seeing differently? Furthermore, who was it that was going to see differently? Was it a different part of me? Would a different me emerge? I knew that I was not going to be able to think my way through this mess, and so there was only one thing to do. Give up trying to understand and go back to the beginning.

In the Beginning

It is a common belief that God, or an Eternal Life Principle or Source, created the universe and all things in it. Some prefer to believe that there is no God and life is just a product of nature; that somehow, we just appeared here, we live and then we die. If we believe that there is a God or Source that created this world as we see and experience it, then it means that God created the good and the bad, life and death. To believe either that God created the world as we know it or that the world is just an accident of nature can lead only to a bleak outlook. Either way we are victims of an all-powerful external source, divine or not, which leaves us helpless and without hope of ever rising above our condition. As neither approach appealed to me, I needed to revisit the nature of my relationship with God.

Having been raised Catholic, for most of my life I thought of God as an inaccessible, all-powerful Being. The God of my youth was distant, judgmental and demanding; He was not gentle, kind and loving. He was, in fact, downright frightening. It certainly never occurred to me that I might talk with Him, even less that He might actually hear, let alone answer, me. That was the job of the priests and the Pope. As good, albeit inherently sinful, Catholics, we were instructed to pray for God's mercy and forgiveness. I must not have been a very good Catholic because I never understood the need for this kind of prayer. As an adult, having failed to make any kind of connection with God, I pushed Him out of the picture completely. God was simply beyond reach. I had a concept of "the universe" as the Source of our existence, but not of God. If there were a God, He would have been busy fixing what was wrong with the world.

Interestingly, although God is mentioned over 2,200 times in the big blue book, I still did not connect with God during the first several years of working with the Course. There was a God, but He remained unreachable. He certainly would not be concerned with my miniscule inconsequential existence. According to what I had learned from the Course, God did not get involved in the affairs of the world. The world was an illusion. I was living as a separated, false self—an ego; therefore, there was no way for me to communicate with God. Besides, the Course states that only a very few can hear God's voice directly and I was not foolish enough to think that I might be among those very few no doubt very holy beings. Again, there was God, Who was far away, and there was me, way down here in the illusion, the sleeping bumbling insignificant self that I was.

As told in *Choosing the Miracle*, in a moment of darkness, when resistance was weak and readiness for receiving help was strong, I was introduced to the teachings of Raj, the voice of Jesus in communion with Paul Tuttle. There is no doubt that I was pointed in that direction because I was ready for it. However, I think I was ready by default, not because I had attained a special level of saintliness. My old familiar belief system had ceased to work, so I had no choice but to give up. Though I may have been ready, this new teaching uprooted everything I thought I understood about everything and anything. "You are smack dab in the middle of the Kingdom of Heaven with your eyes all squinched up saying, 'I cannot see the perfection,'" Raj points out emphatically.

As the Course says, God is. That is the truth. Now I had to deal with it. I thought about Raj's clear presentation of God as our Father and of us, His beloved children. In fact, he invites us to lean into the Father and to release our control over the unfolding of our lives. Since my past learning no longer suited the new direction of my life, I accepted his invitation to refer to God as "my Father" and began to explore the possibility that my life might unfold with more grace if I refrained from interfering with it.

Since I work with people of varied spiritual and religious backgrounds, I long ago adopted a secular approach in my consulting practice. Besides, for many years, I had kept God out of the picture, and so it was easier and more comfortable to leave Him altogether out of the conversation. While I kept my bourgeoning new relationship with God to myself, despite my preference for a neutral approach, references to God eventually trickled into my work with clients. This was not because of any intention on my part to convert others to my way of seeing, but rather as a response to their questions. As had been the case over thirty years of practice, my clients sought clarification regarding the situations in their lives, but now, like me, they too were becoming curious about the more that is here. God came into the conversation with surprising ease and grace in response to questions about the nature of reality. There appeared to be a growing eagerness among people of all walks of life for a healed relationship with their Source. I was not alone in seeking an experience of closeness to God.

Whenever I am confused or uncertain about a situation, I find it helpful to return to the Source. This practice has clarified, simplified and helped resolve many issues. What follows is a thought process that I use in consultation when the need for understanding the foundations of a situation arises and, naturally, when this style of conversation is appropriate. References to God, Allah, Buddha, the Father, Oneness, the Universe or the Eternal Life Principle are used as needed, depending on the client's preferred style of language and symbolism. Sometimes, a word is invented via a metaphor or analogy. In the end, it is not the words that matter, but the meaning behind the words.

If we begin with the premise that there is a Source that can be called God, the Father, the Creator or the Eternal Life Principle from which all of creation emerges, then all of creation must be like this Source. If the Source is whole, invulnerable, complete and eternal, then what is born of this Source must also be whole, invulnerable, complete and eternal. If the nature of the Source is love, Spirit and Pure Mind, then what emanates from this original creative force must be the same. If we are experiencing anything other than the attributes of our Source, then we must be experiencing something that is not true, something that is a dream, an illusion or a fantasy, nothing more than a made-up version of reality.

Many believe that wholeness is something that needs to be developed, acquired or earned, and that health, wellness and abundance is up to us. But in a frame of reference in which all is of God, these beliefs are baseless. The truth is that wholeness, wellness and abundance are our birthright. We may have pretended for a while that we could be something else, but that is not what is true about us. Our true starting point is eternal love which is reflected in perfect wholeness.

Who or What Am I?

With this new perspective, I felt I had been given a new lease on life, but now I didn't know what this life would entail. It seemed as though each time a new level of clarity was reached, a completely new set of questions arose. If I wasn't going to disappear into the vast nothingness beyond the illusion, then there must be an "I," in some form, to whom Jesus had addressed his big blue book. Who was that I? What was that I?

Of course, the best place to learn about the truth is in the middle of the classroom of life, especially after having joined with guidance. As I was reminded by my friend, "The ego will use what you do in the world to confuse you. Its only goal is to keep you fixated on the world. It uses what you do because doing is of the ego. Being is of God. When you are not fixated on what you are doing, you are in a better position to be peaceful and quiet and to allow Being, to allow God Being through you. This is why when you have 'nothing to do' you feel lost and you look for something to do."

Well, my life was filled with things to do, among them, my work with clients and my writing. Naturally, the ego-identified part of my mind did its best to weaken my resolve to pursue this journey of awakening, and one of its favourite targets was my writing. Somehow, it always managed to find a way to make me feel guilty by virtue of my incompetence and ignorance. Any little error in my publications, any criticism of my writing, was magnified a thousand times, causing me on a number of occasions to want to quit writing altogether. I had made some editorial changes to one of my books, but still, I was unable to make peace with it. *Please help me see this differently*, I said to Jesus. He offered up a few words of wisdom.

"Either way, from the perspective of the ego, you are not content with the book. Peace and contentment will not be found through what you do in the world, ever. I also told you that your ego would use your writing to confuse and upset you, and this is what it is doing. It uses what you are doing; writing is what you are doing. Doing is of the ego. In the end, it never matters what you do in the world. Focus on being in the Presence of God. What needs to be done in the world will come to you, peacefully, quietly. It will not be out of conflict nor will it be a means to resolve conflict in the world. There is only one conflict, and that is your imagined battle with God. If you are seemingly in conflict with something in the world, seemingly divided or uncertain, it is simply a reflection of your uncertainty about God, about your wholeness. The only conflict is your battle to remain a separate individual, apart from the Father. That is the only conflict that needs to be addressed, questioned and healed."

It seemed to me that what I had done, actually, all of what I was doing in the world was very real, very tangible. I could not ignore the seeming reality of life in a body, even if I knew, at least intellectually, the truth of my nature as spirit. When I still could not let go of the feelings of guilt and inadequacy about my work, I once again asked for help.

"The difficult part is to understand that this is not the real you. The one you identify with as a person in a body, in the world, interacting with other bodies in the world, with specific character traits is not the real you. The real you is still at Home with God and has never left. The real you is whole and cannot and does not make any mistakes.

"This is the same for everyone you encounter. Everyone is acting out a role, playing a part that is not their real Self. Everyone is pretending to be what they are not. How can you blame, attack or withhold love from somebody who is pretending? Everyone is just acting out. If they were in their Right Mind, if they were coming from the level of their wholeness, their actions would be whole, kind, gentle and, above all, loving. This is where everyone is, though this may not be where they believe themselves to be.

"In order for you to remain in this state of ignorance, which is really not your real state, you must have a good reason to not question it. It appears real. Your senses tell you there is pain, there are survival needs to be attended to, you need food, water, air to breathe; all these things keep you busy and focused outside of your mind. You are literally out of your mind. It is only in your mind that you can try an alternative way of seeing things. This is what is called a leap of faith; you have the faith that perhaps there is something else. A leap of faith does not mean believing that you can have a better dream in the world if you believe in yourself and the world. There are no needs in the place of wholeness; there is no hunger, no want and no lack in the place that you have never left, in your true home in the Kingdom of Heaven.

"In the place you have never left, there is only Being, Being God's Expression, God Being through you. You must abandon your affiliation with the small insignificant imaginary self, a self that you believe to be very real. A leap of faith is required in order to question, is that all there is? Is this everything that I can be? If I can be more than this separated self, what is my true Self? What does it look like? This Self is God Being you, since all there is in Reality is God, God Being. So you can be nothing more and nothing less than God Being."

If the "real" me is still at home with God, what is the me that is here, in the illusion? What does it mean to be a child of God, to be an expression of what God is being?

"You think you are a separated daughter, a child of God who is an individual, different from the Father, but that is an impossibility. So what you think you are is made up. You are a divine child of God—God's Expression. But somehow, you have decided that it is better to pretend to be something else, a little self, an independent thinker, separate from the One Mind, with an independent will. You have convinced yourself of this so completely that you have forgotten the truth of who you are and you are afraid of what will happen should you relinquish this false, small self.

"What you don't realize is that by relinquishing the false self, you naturally and automatically become your true Self and you remember that you are God's Expression. That is the truth. It is simple. It does not require extensive learning, study or practice. It simply requires the willingness to accept the possibility that it might be true. Accept the possibility that instead of the small self that you believe yourself to be, you are really the whole Self that God created, right now, not in some distant future. All that is needed is that you let go of the lie, the lie with which you are so comfortable and familiar, but which obscures the truth of who you really are.

"Somewhere on your journey, a senseless journey, as we have already pointed out, you encountered a teaching that stated that the attainment of your Christhood—your wholeness as an Expression of God—is something that would require thousands of lifetimes. Because you were studying with your wrong mind, the ego, whose only intent is to protect its existence, you accepted this teaching as true. You established for yourself a tremendously high bar of attainment, one that was nearly impossible to attain and one that was certainly not encouraging, if not outright depressing.

"If only God is, right now, then all is God's Expression, God's Creation. You are God's Creation, not just a child who foolishly makes mistakes. You are the Christ, whole, as God is creating you now. Creation is not something that happened long ago, in the past; it is not something that you need to run after to reconnect with. God creates *now*. Time is a concept of the ego. If God creates now and you are God's Creation, then you are whole, perfect, the Christ *now*. If you do not know or see this now, it is because you persist in using perception or limited seeing; you prefer to hold on to an idea of a separate self as opposed to knowing and experiencing the truth of perfect Oneness."

> Beyond this world there is a world I want. I choose to see that world instead of this, for here is nothing that I really want. (ACIM.W.129)

God and Me

The biggest shock in my learning came when it finally hit home that there is only one Mind—the Mind of God—and that I am a thought, just a thought, in the Mind of God, and that only God's Will is real. I had spent a lifetime building, cultivating and nurturing my independence, only to learn that, not only was it not worth diddly-squat, it actually did not accomplish anything in reality. Nothing can come between God and His Creations, and all of His Creations are an expression of His Will.

Very simply, if I wanted to experience what God Wills for me, I needed to relinquish the made-up self and all of its false definitions and allow what is whole and eternal to simply *be* in me. If God is Being me, then whatever I do independently from the Father is meaningless, at least insofar as reality is concerned. In truth, I have no control over who or what I am. My existence is an expression of the Will of God. My existence has nothing to do with any efforts or desires on my part.

The implications of this revelation were more far-reaching than anything I had ever before considered. It meant that my entire existence as I knew it had been little more than a sham, a cover-up of the truth of what I truly am. For a split second, I experienced a terrifyingly absolute darkness in which I came face to face with the imminent annihilation of me. In that moment, God appeared as the most fearsome of beings. I had two choices: accept the truth, take hold of the hand of Jesus and trust that I was moving in the right direction, or ignore it and continue to maintain the illusion with my old teacher, the ego. In that moment, I invited God into my life and I took the first step in the right direction.

During my daily walks, I had adopted the practice of looking for what God is Being in everything that caught my eye. I was curious about what it would mean to see the Kingdom of Heaven no matter where I was. In time, I began to see God in acts of kindness, a loving touch between a mother and child, a smile for no reason, the joyful chirping of chickadees in the trees, a beautiful early spring flower pushing through the winter-hardened ground.

I even recognized His Presence in my own mind when I forgot to judge a brother, when I took the time to wonder what I might see. It was while on such a walk that I asked once more, what is God Being right now? The answer came readily and easily, with an unwavering knowing that filled me with such warmth and profound joy that I was brought to tears.

God is Being *me*!

Huh!

God is Being me!

Very simply, if we wish to experience what God Wills for us, all we need is to relinquish the made-up self and all of its false definitions and allow what is whole and eternal to simply *be* in us.

If you ask the question now as you read these words, what is God Being right now? The answer can only be that God is Being *you*.

Chapter 4

The Hand of God

> You are but asked to let the future go, and place it in God's Hands. And you will see by your experience that you have laid the past and present in His Hands as well, because the past will punish you no more, and future dread will now be meaningless. (ACIM.W.194)

The year 2012 was the final one in a nine-year cycle for me, perhaps the most significant nine years of my life. I know, I know, there is no hierarchy of important years, or months or days, for that matter. Whether we are aware of it or not, the truth is that each moment of our lives is perfect in that it holds all that is needed for the complete unfolding of our Being. Still, there are those periods when the evidence of this unfolding as experienced through revelation seems to leap to our awareness, taking us completely by surprise, even causing us to stumble and fall as long-held ancient beliefs crumble beneath our feet. These moments force us to reach beyond the safety of failing familiar frontiers, leaving us open to awakening to what has been there all along.

We are told that awakening is a natural process, a return to our normal, real condition—awakening is in fact our birthright. It is immediately available and very much within our reach. What is surprising is how tightly we cling to the ignorance that covers up our true state as perfect, wholly loved sons and daughters of God. It does not matter that we are rewarded for our faithful obedience to this ignorance with sickness, pain, suffering and death. Still, we stubbornly cling. Also surprising—though it shouldn't be— is how simple awakening is, how uncomplicated and close at hand it is; in truth, being our natural condition, it has never left us. In fact, personal effort of any kind is likely to interfere with what is a wholly natural process, an unfolding that is occurring whether or not we are actively engaging it. All that is required is the willingness to consider that this might be the truth. How pleasant it is to discover—even in the tiniest of glimpses—how lusciously sublime it feels to awaken to the Love that has always been and will always remain the Source of our very being.

Such was the climate of the start of that particular 9 year, a fitting finale for an intense period of study, reflection, undoing and relearning—a graduation of sorts—a state of mind and heart ready for an experience of the movement of what God is Being. The countless times I had counselled clients about the nature of the 9 Personal Year came back to haunt me like an all-too-familiar television commercial: it's time to downsize, unload, release the past and make room for new directions and experiences. Most importantly, it is a time to rest.

Many of my clients request numerology consultations during periods of crisis or transition, very often experienced in the 9 year. As I wrote in my numerology blog, this is indeed a time of release and, as such, requires an attitude of surrender in order for the necessary changes to take place. Since most of us are programmed to be self-reliant, independent thinking and autonomous, yielding to the flow of change can be difficult. For some, it can be very frightening; for others, seemingly downright impossible. In most cases, the greater the demand for change, the greater the feelings of uncertainty, doubt, anxiety, stress and fear. In time, these changes are recognized as having been appropriate, sometimes even divinely inspired, often acting as bridges leading to further unfolding. In time, a little more of our eing is uncovered and embraced.

Change requires letting go of habits and familiar, usually all-too-comfortable ways of thinking, being and doing. Change requires the relinquishment of control and the abandonment of old beliefs. Just as one would not prevent an eleven-month-old child from taking those first steps that would lead her to leave behind her crawling days, we must allow our spirits to guide us beyond our own thresholds. This requires faith in an inner wisdom that knows what is best for us, the belief that we are worthy of experiencing more of our Being and trust that we will be given the support that we need as we stumble out of our temporary darkness into the light of awakening. As might be expected, the greater the call for change, the greater the need for trust. The more resistance we muster up, the more difficult and uncomfortable the process. As we yield more and more to the movement of change, the experience grows easier, more graceful and more enjoyable.

Apparently not immune to the cycles of time and transformation, I too would be required to experience some letting go—some significant letting go, as it turned out. A glaring outward expression of this process of relinquishment came in the form of the decision to sell my house and move to a condo—a fitting parallel for the deeper inner business of letting go that would be occurring at the same time. My deep desire to awaken to my true reality in the Kingdom of Heaven would require the complete relinquishment of my addiction and attachment to, among many other attachments, my substitute home in the dream. This was indeed a time of endings. Big time! While nearly a decade earlier I had boldly set out to make peace with God, little did I know what the journey would entail. Looking back, it became clear that the journey had barely begun. Perhaps if I had known that I would encounter my darkest demons and most profound fears on the way to making peace with God, I might have been frightened out of my worthy pursuit. For that small mercy, I will remain forever grateful, for I know with absolute certainty that all has unfolded as it was meant to.

In the fall of 2011, a sign for a new condo project went up on the lot of a church I occasionally passed while on my daily walks. If I were ever to move to a condo—something I had begun to consider—this would be the perfect place. Situated near the water, across the street from a grocery store, in walking distance to the train and bus terminal and sufficiently tucked away from the noise of traffic to be very quiet and private, it was an ideal location. My guess was that it was going to be far too expensive for my humble means. A few weeks later, the sign had disappeared, and so I gave it no further thought. In January, a real estate agent attended one of my numerology workshops. It just so happened that she had been temporarily assigned to that very same project. The sign had been removed but the condo project was moving forward.

After careful consideration and consultation with my financial planner, I concluded that it was indeed the right move. It felt right, and I was ready for the change. It made sense both logistically and financially; it was in harmony with my numerology cycles and, given the low mortgage rates, the timing was right for selling the house. I submitted an offer on the south-facing corner unit on the third floor, the one I felt would be just perfect, the one that had first caught my eye. It had a huge corner balcony that would be ideal for setting up an outdoor workspace during the summer months, plenty of sunlight for flowers and herbs, high enough for a sweeping view of trees and open sky and angled just right to catch both sunrise and sunset. It was perfect.

If I needed further proof in support of my bold decision, there was the ease and swiftness with which paperwork, banking, financing—all areas well beyond my field of expertise, or interest, for that matter—were processed. Oh, and there was also the interesting fact that the property had been previously owned by the clergy and had served as a retirement home for the Fathers of Saint Viateur. Somehow, that was a further indicator of the rightness of the decision. The entire matter was resolved in a fortnight, with very little to do on my part to make it happen, and so I truly felt not only guided, but also very much supported. I could continue to focus my attention on being in the Presence of God, and the complicated things of the world would be taken care of... Except that, in the middle of what was a surprisingly smooth business transaction, I decided to concede to murmurs from concerned family members suggesting that I approach the matter responsibly, that I should not be so impulsive and that I should engage in a little more research. And so it was that I subcontracted that part of the job to my ever-so-ready and actually very willing, no doubt by then, chomping-at-the-bit, independent-thinking ego-self, which was only too happy to send me on a wild goose chase. I spent the better part of the days it took for the business end to be completed in search of the better deal, the better location or whatever the ego could cook up to foster doubt in my original, clearly inspired decision. This was a perfect opportunity to stir up a little hesitation and uncertainty, mixed in with a sprinkling of fear and anxiety. Enough of this time spent being in the Presence of God—there was a brand new drama to stir up in the dream!

Perhaps I should consider renting instead of buying, the voice for confusion chimed in. Maybe I should take the less-expensive unit on the second floor or the larger first-floor unit facing the water or the middle unit on the third floor so I could have more wall space for bookcases. How about the corner unit on the northwest corner with a view of the water and, wait—what about the other new condo development up the street with the crown mouldings and propane fireplaces? Then there was the question of what to do with all my belongings! These two-bedroom condos were two-thirds the size of my bungalow, not counting the fully finished and furnished basement. Yikes! At one point, the real estate agent had four units set aside in my name pending acceptance of my offer, no doubt having decided that it was simpler to just hold them all while I sorted out the mess in my mind.

I suppose I could have been excited about all this business, but the more time and thought I invested in the matter, the more anxious and uncertain I became. After decades of instability and far too many changes of residence, I had sworn off moving for the rest of my life. Only half-jokingly, I frequently declared that they would have to scrape me off the floor of my beloved bungalow. Yet, there was no denying that selling the house and moving to a condo made perfect sense; something I reminded myself of many times. It was a financially sound decision, and very practical in that it would simplify my life considerably, freeing me to focus on writing, work with clients and travel. Even though there was no doubt that this had been a guided and, therefore, right decision, being that it was such an important one, it was filled with grist for the ego's mill of confusion.

I rest in God. (ACIM.W.109)

One night, exhausted from too many days and nights of this frenzied, peace-nullifying research, I settled down for my evening meditation. *Enough!* I declared. This hunt for the better condo had not only worn down my reserve of peace, it had sucked my attention right out into the world, away from that place in my mind that was always just a thought away from being in the Presence of God, a place I had grown very fond of. *This isn't working*, I said to God, to Jesus and to whomever might be listening. *I've had enough.* Surely, I had been guided to the place where I was supposed to be; at the very least, this is what I chose to believe. I just wanted to allow this change to unfold as smoothly as possible, as it was meant to unfold. No more doubting, no more searching, no more second-guessing myself, no more confusion. *Enough, enough! This is not where I want my attention to be focused. I want to return it to being in the Presence of God. Let Thy Will—not mine—be done!*

Sometime during that night I experienced what was like a very vivid dream, only I don't think it was a dream because it felt far more real than a dream. Nevertheless, my eyes were closed and I was, essentially, seemingly asleep. In a heightened state of peaceful awareness, I was aware that I was lying on my right side, resting comfortably and very peacefully, without a care in the world, like a child taking an afternoon nap. It was a state of perfectly balanced, warm and safe, yet somehow conscious, rest. Then I became aware that I was not lying on my bed at all; instead, I was floating in space, my body cradled in a luscious, luminescent green leaf that pulsed gently with nurturing, soothing life force. I lay in total and complete comfort and joy, with tears streaming down my face as I realized with absolute certainty that I rested in the Hand of God.

As much as I would have wanted to remain in that exquisite state of perfect peace and safety for the remainder of my days, I knew better than to attempt to cling to what was still just a taste of what awaits us upon awakening. The ego-identified self was not about to stand by and welcome my awakening without a struggle; in fact, it was going to dig deep and do whatever it needed to ensure its survival. Nonetheless, over the months that followed, whenever uncertainty arose concerning the house or the condo, I recalled as best as I could the memory of the beautiful leaf and the feeling of total, utter safety that comes when we relinquish all self-governing actions and yield to the Love of our Father.

Thus was the stage set for that 9 year of endings: with a move from my lovely bungalow, the home in which I had resided for the longest period of my life, combined with a shifting of awareness from a world of illusions to our true reality in the Kingdom of Heaven. This tale of two realities would be reflected in the parallel events surrounding the sale of the house and preparations for the move to condo living, and the undoing of ego-structures and false beliefs as I journeyed toward awakening to Reality. One would entail the letting go of long-held lifestyle habits and adjusting to a smaller kitchen, abandoning my beloved garden and giving up possessions that would not fit in the smaller space. The other would require the releasing of lifelong habits of perception and thinking, deeply engrained "self" definitions and beliefs that had served me well for a while, but that I had clearly outgrown.

All of this change and shift necessitated complete trust. On the one hand, I had to trust that the condo would be built on schedule, that I would really like it—something that was important to me— and that the house would be sold on time. On the other hand, I had to trust that awakening was within reach, that there was life after the end of illusions and that I wouldn't just disappear into some endless nothingness. I felt as though I had jumped off the far edge of the world into the vast unknown, and only the memory of the Hand of God kept the terror away.

Oh, and yes, in the end, I did settle for the condo on the corner on the third floor, the one that had first caught my attention, or, more precisely, the one that had called to me.

Chapter 5

Walking Meditations

Now we are sure we do not walk alone. For God is here, and with Him all our brothers. Now we know that we will never lose the way again. (ACIM.M.75)

Walking with God

A few people have asked if I would write up or make a recording of what I call, for lack of a better term, my "walking meditations." These could just as easily have been called walking contemplations, moving awareness, walking prayerfulness or, simply, the practice of paying attention. I believe the key element of this practice is that while walking, I find myself to be in a particularly receptive state, being in an environment over which I have little control, not knowing who I will meet along the way, what I will see or what I will experience. My only function while walking is to pay attention, which is the true function of mind. Being free of expectations, pre-conceptions or concerns of any kind, the mind that pays attention is ready to experience what is there.

As much as I might have liked to come up with a formula for these walking meditations, in the end I concluded that to apply a structured or systematic approach would defeat the purpose of the exercise. Instead, I will share a few of my experiences; perhaps they will inspire you to tune into your deepest inner knowing for the method or approach that works best for you. All that is needed is a quiet mind and an openness to seeing what is really there.

As shared in *Choosing the Miracle*, in the summer of 2011, I was very clearly guided to set down my MP3 player and go for my daily walks in a state of quiet, undistracted openness and receptivity.

My love affair with headphones and listening devices went back decades to those periods in my life when, during difficult times or when I felt out of sorts, I found peace and a return to my centre by listening to music. When I became a student of *A Course in Miracles*, music was replaced by hundreds of hours of lectures from Course teacher Kenneth Wapnick. Over the years, I wore out several cassette, CD and MP3 players.

Although this practice served the purpose of helping me to find peace and satisfy my seemingly endless thirst for knowledge, ultimately it reinforced the unhealthy habit of isolation. While I was plugged in, I was not tuned in to what was going on around me. In fact, I was very much sheltered from everything outside of my personal space. For having abided by the guidance to give up this isolating practice, I have been rewarded with some of the most wonderful experiences of joining and greater awareness, perhaps the best experiences for validating the teachings of a lifetime spent learning.

> God is with me. He is my Source of life, the life within, the air I breathe, the food by which I am sustained, the water which renews and cleanses me. He is my home, wherein I live and move; the Spirit which directs my actions, offers me Its Thoughts, and guarantees my safety from all pain. He covers me with kindness and with care, and holds in love the Son He shines upon, who also shines on Him. How still is he who knows the truth of what He speaks today! (ACIM.W.222)

When I was guided to walk in silence, to walk with God, I understood not only that I was to leave my MP3 player and headphones on the desk, but that I was to go with a quiet, open mind. I must admit that at first I felt somewhat lost, even naked or exposed. What would I pay attention to if I were not listening to a lecture? Would I be bored? What would I see? There were people out there in the world beyond the safety of my headphones. Would I be required to interact with them?

While on that first headphone-free walk, I contemplated the thought that God is here, now. I reminded myself that God is the air that I breathe, that God is in everything and every being. God is in the sidewalk, the grass and the trees; the road, the cars and the stores. As I allowed myself to be curious to know what this meant, to feel the truth, a sense of deep peace came over me.

It was business as usual when I turned onto the busy boulevard that took me to my favourite grocery stores, with no shortage of people and things in my field of awareness. Cars, delivery trucks and buses flowed up and down the boulevard, while brothers and sisters scurried about their business. As I walked and let myself into this flow of life, I became filled with a deep sense of the movement of God's Creation—an all-enveloping joy and love and feeling of safety and endless beauty that flowed through and around everyone and everything. As I stood in awe at the intersection waiting for the crossing signal, I was overcome by a deep knowing that filled every fibre of my being—God was right here, right now. I let the tears flow behind the large sunglasses that had become an important part of my walking attire.

While out for another walk, as I wound my way through the quiet streets of my residential neighbourhood, admiring the beautiful gardens and soaking in the warmth of the sun, I asked Jesus how I would see the Kingdom of Heaven.

"You won't see the Kingdom of Heaven with the body's eyes; you will know it with your heart."

Thank goodness for large sunglasses, I thought, as I continued on my way, letting the tears flow.

It was only while working on this chapter that it occurred to me that the intersection of these busy boulevards where I have since experienced a number of moments of closeness to God, has a very interesting pair of names: "Des Sources" and "Pierrefonds" can be translated as "from the Source" and "bedrock." Who would have thought that concrete, asphalt and moving chunks of steel could inspire a sublime experience of the Presence of God!

Breaking the Isolation

Being a practical person, I like to combine my walking meditations with an errand or two, no matter how small. In fact, running an errand brings the process of being in the Presence of God into the mundane, into the present moment, bridging the gap between Heaven and earth. When I first began this practice, I must admit that I felt somewhat uncomfortable. What do you do when you're not listening to music or a lecture? What do you do when you're paying attention to what's going on outside of you or around you?

"You look at people, you pay attention, you look into their eyes," my friend responded. "Smile," he urged. "You have a nice smile. Share it."

Right. Me? Smile at a stranger, for no reason? This was going to be a serious act of breaking the isolation. It was not that I didn't like to interact with others; I had met thousands of people through consultations and business networking, interactions that I had thoroughly enjoyed. Only, I also liked my private, quiet space. But I had a new teacher now, so there was only one thing to do, especially that I was walking without the protective shield of my headset and MP3 player. As suggested, I began the practice of looking at people and smiling. At first, the smiles I attempted were shy and self-conscious. On one sunny afternoon, while turning the corner at my familiar holy intersection, I heard clearly, "Show some teeth!"

Okay, I thought, and as my attention came to a shabbily dressed old man sitting alone on a bench next to the bus stop, I smiled. I showed him a full set of teeth. To my surprise, he smiled right back at me, and as our eyes met, I felt our Souls join in loving recognition. More than that, beyond what my physical eyes perceived, I saw in my brother only great beauty, which could only be an Expression of what the Father was Being in him. From that moment on I always smiled with a full set of teeth.

Along with the inspiring and profound experiences of walking in the Presence of God, there have also been humorous encounters. Like the time when an older man who was approaching me from the opposite direction caught my attention. As I began to smile, he quickly reached out his hand, which I took in a firm handshake—easy enough to do with my big mitts.

"I'm from India. You from?" he said.

With our hands still gripped in a warm shake, I answered, "I'm from here."

"What country you from?" he asked again.

I have a hint of Oriental features that throws people off when I tell them I am Canadian; strains of past life incarnations seeping through, I usually say. Thinking that he too might be a bit baffled, I replied, "Canada, from Quebec."

"You alone?" he asked.

"No, I have a lot of people around me," I answered quickly, sensing that this encounter could be headed in an awkward direction.

"You not alone?" He made a side-to-side move with his head that suggested that I might be with someone, but open to exploring possibilities. It seemed as though he was fishing to see if my imaginary marital status might be shaky enough to welcome a new companion.

"No," I smiled, my status still unchanged. Besides, I was never *really* alone. When I was able to retrieve my hand, I wished him a wonderful day and off I went.

We crossed paths again several days later, this time, heading in opposite directions. I had finished running errands and was on my way home, so with full bags dangling from each hand, a handshake was not possible—though a big toothy smile was.

"Where you from?" he began, apparently having forgotten all about our first encounter.

"Right here," I replied. I'm not sure where his mind was at, but his heart was in the right place. There was a boyish simplicity about the man that said life is here, now, for the taking and it filled my heart with joy. After a brief friendly exchange, I wished him a lovely day and we parted ways.

Get Me to the Church on Time

It was a wonderful Sunday morning in August, a perfect day for a walk, I thought, as I stepped out of the house. I breathed in the fresh air deeply and let the warm sunlight wash over me. As I turned my attention to being in the Presence of God, I asked, *What is God's purpose for me today as I go for this walk?*

As usual, I had an errand to run. Maybe I'd pick up some cucumbers for my salad, perhaps a couple of zucchinis, nothing important. Somehow, I still clung to the idea that I should have a plan, no matter how inconsequential it might be. Having a direction in which to move had always given a sense of orderliness to life. Although the need for self-defined orderliness and planning was rapidly waning, I knew that it was okay to employ familiar means while I practised shifting to my bourgeoning new way of seeing and being. One day I would walk forth in all areas of my life with no plan whatsoever, guided only by the awareness of the Will of the Father.

When I turned the corner in front of the church, I caught sight of a man diagonally across the street stopped on the sidewalk and looking in my direction. He held his palm across his chest in a gesture that might have suggested that—had I been a little vainer—he had fallen into a swoon at the sight of my great beauty. I know, I'm indulging in a little poetic license, but I was told to have fun with my writing! He was a small man, of Mediterranean origin—possibly Italian, mid to late sixties, I guessed. He remained standing, without moving, as I crossed the street toward him. I wondered if there was cause for concern, if perhaps he might be lost. So I gave him the big broad smile I had become accustomed to sharing and stopped to see if I might be of assistance.

"Hello," he said somewhat feebly.

Concerned, I asked if he was okay, pointing to the hand on his chest. He appeared to be having difficulty breathing. He nodded briefly and took a laboured breath.

"Breathe," I told him, and I took a long, slow deep breath along with him. We took a few more breaths together, and though he appeared very calm, I remained concerned. Ready to walk him home or get the car if need be, I asked if he was going far.

With his free hand, he pointed across the street. "C-h-o-o-c-h," he said.

I looked over my shoulder toward where he was pointing and realized that he was not lost; rather, he was on his way to Sunday Mass. I nodded toward the church.

"Yes," he said smiling.

If his breathing had not returned to normal, I would have walked him across the street to his destination. But he seemed at peace and quite content to go on his way. "Go with Jesus," I said. "He'll take good care of you."

He smiled back, and as I continued on my way, I knew that Jesus had been right there with us. After a few paces, I turned back to see if he needed help only to find him scooting right across the street like a youngster. On my way home from my walk, I dropped into the store near the church for a second try at finding zucchinis. There was my Mediterranean friend, laughing and chatting with someone, seemingly in fine form, no doubt having been taken care of by Jesus.

The Beauty of God Being

It had been a hot summer, and the previous couple of days of rain and thunderstorms had done little to clear away the mass of hot air that clung like an unwelcome guest. The cicadas were singing with gusto, forecasting yet another very hot mid-August day. When I awoke that day, my first thoughts were of the work that needed to be done in the next few weeks in order to prepare the house before I could put it up for sale. There were mouldings that needed painting, a bathroom door in the basement that needed a coat of paint and a list of other things to do, but I decided that I didn't feel like putting my attention on home renovations. Instead, I wanted to continue my ongoing contemplation of what God was Being here, now, curious to know what the world was really like as God is Being it, in all its beauty and grace and orderliness. I thought about how my perception and, in fact, my entire experience would change as

I abandoned my personal definitions of what I see around me, as I abandoned the meanings that I had given everything I see. It is only then that God would reveal to me what He is Being now.

It was with these thoughts that I stepped out of the house to run an errand that hot mid-August morning. As I reached the corner at the end of my street, I was greeted by a trio of painted lady butterflies lifting off the concrete just a couple of paces ahead of my sandaled feet. Two more butterflies fluttered about the now flower-less pair of magnolias that spread their generous branches on the corner lot. As I continued, now more attentive to where I was placing my steps, more butterflies opened their wings and fluttered up from the concrete as though emerging out of the ether. More butterflies rose and fluttered and danced and turned about me as I walked in sheer delight, and I knew that this was a first-hand experience of what God was Being. I had walked the same street, the same sidewalk, hundreds of times over the previous 15 years, but I do not recall ever seeing so many butterflies. In fact, I do not recall ever seeing so many butterflies in a single place. I resisted the tears, not wanting to walk into the store a sobbing mess. Instead, I smiled and revelled in the beauty, the harmony, the life through which—in which—I walked, and in which I knew we were loved.

With each block I passed, I expected that my new friends would scatter but they remained. Other than the twenty- or thirty-foot detour I made to avoid the groundhog that was happily sunning itself at the edge of the sidewalk, I was accompanied by my winged friends most of the way to the store. On the way home, though grateful for the experience and not wanting to press my luck, I hoped that my friends would be there again. As I moved away from the noise of the main boulevard onto the quieter streets of my neighbourhood, the butterflies re-emerged. Again, they danced about as we walked home together; again, I gave wide berth to the groundhog that seemed oblivious to the fact that he was right in the middle of a city. My beautiful winged friends accompanied me all the way home, with one settling on a golden yellow black-eyed Susan in the flower bed next to my front door. This time I let the tears flow. There is beauty in life. And life is of God. And God is here now.

A Moment in Eternity

In one of our chats, Jesus had pointed out that I thought that if everything was perfect and whole, then everything, that is, what God is Being, or life in the Kingdom of Heaven, would be dull and undifferentiated. "That's really very funny," he said. "That means you believe that in order for there to be interest and beauty, there must be ugliness and imperfection. To be able to appreciate the truth of what is there, you must first relinquish your personal definitions of what beauty, order, harmony and perfection are. Only then can you experience true beauty and perfection."

While out for another afternoon walk, peaceful mind once again intact, I renewed my commitment to being curious about what God is Being in the world around me. It was mild and sunny, another perfect day. My favourite holy intersection was alive with the stop and go of cars and trucks, a popular attraction on that corner being the Tim Hortons serving up fresh java to patrons needing a midday caffeine fix. It was on the return trip from the grocery store, with my knapsack filled with fresh veggies for my evening salad that I encountered a small bottleneck on the sidewalk, where several people waited for the city bus to come to a full stop.

Two ladies sipping take-out coffee were carrying on an intense conversation next to the bus shelter; a couple of students from the nearby high school stood in their own private spaces near the curb, attention fixated on hand-held devices; a woman in Islamic attire, eyes cast downward, waited by the shelter entrance; a man of medium stature walked intently toward us. Each person was absorbed by the concerns of his or her personal life drama, so there was little opportunity to make contact and share a smile. All of us were converging on the same spot, the spot I would need to cross, since I was not taking the bus, the spot at which those descending the bus and those behind me and coming from inside the bus shelter would necessarily need to cross. All moved in a purposeful, self-contained and orderly manner.

Normally, I would have excused myself, perhaps in both official languages, *pardon, excuse me*, so I could pass through the small crowd without bumping into anyone with my full knapsack. Instead, I decided to halt, mid-stride and simply yield to the moment. What is God Being here, now? While each person moved before, around and beside me, off the bus and onto the bus, flowing by me as though I did not exist, though separate from each other in form, I sensed an exquisite tingling that was not of the body. In that moment, I recognized that we were all joined as one in spirit. In peaceful stillness, I allowed the movement of Life in all of its splendid colours and hues to pour Itself around and inside me, and as I opened myself up to the full experience of this movement, it was as though I had stopped in time and space while the rest of the world flowed around me. In that quiet, defenceless stillness, I became aware of the harmonious current of the ever-present Life force that we all share, an aliveness that carried a faint, though distinctly sweet scent, a delightful melody, an almost sensual warmth and an undeniable sense of safety and rightness.

The entire scene could not have taken more than half a minute—as passengers disembarked, new passengers embarked and the congestion dissipated—but it was a half-minute I would gladly have extended into hours, into eternity. Though far too brief, it was a half-minute that convinced me beyond a shadow of a doubt that awakening to the full awareness of the movement of All that is Being at any given moment was going to be a truly wonderful experience. Once again, I reminded myself that, since what God is Being is always new, this moment would not likely be repeated. Nonetheless, I would always remember the experience and relish the memory, but, more importantly, I could look forward to what other new experiences would come as I entrusted more and more of my experience to the Father.

Walking Meditations for All Seasons

If you think that being in the Presence of God occurs only on beautiful, sunny summer days, think again—although, in the end, it is best not to think at all!

Everyone has experienced wonder in some form at some point in their life, if only in their childhood: the child sitting on the porch entranced by the lovely white flakes falling from Heaven, the fiery red sky over the horizon as the sun sets, the sound of a dry leaf underfoot or the curious dexterity of a caterpillar turning over in the grass. This is the same wonder that we are being asked to invite into our new way of seeing. It is the attitude that will enable us to see what is really going on in the moment.

There was an inch of fresh snow on the ground, but beneath it were patches of thick ice. We were experiencing a brief respite after severe cold conditions and I decided to go for a walk. The snow was light, but with each step that I took, I slipped a half step back.

"Slow down, pay attention," I heard my friend say. And I did, which is when I noticed that my body was tense from attempting to stay vertical and not slip on the ice. It was true, there was no need to hurry but I was in the habit of walking at a rather fast pace. So I slowed down and took in the beauty of the snow-covered ground, the trees and the rooftops. As I carefully placed one booted-foot on the ground, and then another, it occurred to me that, not only was I walking on the ground, the same ground was Mother Earth. As I stilled my mind and paid attention to each step, a deep calm came over me. With each step I took, I knew that Mother Earth was reaching up and supporting me and I was safe and, above all, I was loved.

'Who walks with me?' This question should be asked a thousand times a day, till certainty has ended doubting and established peace. Today let doubting cease. God speaks for you in answering your question with these words:

I walk with God in perfect holiness.

I light the world, I light my mind and all the minds which God created one with me. (ACIM.W.156)

Chapter 6

Full Circle

To every thing there is a season, and a time to every purpose under the heaven. (Ecclesiastes 3:1)

Downsizing

Before I could set one foot into my new condo, I needed to unload some of my cherished possessions. Having moved over a dozen times in my life, organizing, sorting and packing assorted possessions were activities that fell well within my range of expertise. Besides, this move was going to be easier than all the others were since I was moving to a smaller space and I didn't have to worry about settling my daughters into new rooms. Although some serious downsizing was called for, I was confident in my ability to make it happen in an orderly fashion. I was actually looking forward to the move, as it was an activity that catered to my penchant for orderliness—it was something that made me feel competent, productive and effective.

I began the lengthy process of sorting through cupboards full of dishes of all kinds, deciding which I would keep. I could bring only what was necessary—a few serving plates and baking dishes, one set of wine glasses and dishes, and basic utensils. I kept the tablecloths and placemats I liked best and gave away those I held onto for that one day, maybe, that never came. I cleared out seldom-used closets, gave away clothes I had not worn in years and moved what remained into a single closet. Since I had the architectural floor plan of the condo, I knew how much space I would have for all of my household and personal items—not much! There were shelves in the furnace room that served as storage for my daughters, empty computer equipment boxes, jars and containers, Christmas decorations and wrapping materials, tools and renovation materials and on and on—none of which would make the move to the condo. I took photos of the items I wanted to sell or donate, wrote up descriptions, took measurements where appropriate, and posted them on the Internet.

I put several bookcases for sale, which meant that I had to give up many of my most prized possessions—books. Though a task that might have appeared difficult at first, it turned out that I was able to give away boxes of books simply because I really had no inclination to read them again. This was particularly the case with the more esoteric and metaphysical works on my shelves. I picked up each book, asked myself if I would read it again and then set it aside either to be given away or packed for the condo. Astrology and numerology texts, *Course in Miracles*-related books, cookbooks, reference and technical books were among those that survived the great purge. All those books, all those words, all that information, only to come to the conclusion that I really don't know shit. One thing I did know was that I was done with the studying and the learning.

Occasionally, doubts arose. Would I like my new life? Would I regret this radical decision? Had I made a mistake? In response to my online ads, strangers began to stream to my door, picking up items they had just purchased, each time taking with them a piece of my past, leaving a little more empty space in their wake. I wondered what my new life would be like and especially if I would be happy with it. Somehow, that was very important to me at this time of my life. Parallel to the move to the condo, there was the matter of the move from the state of the dream to the state of awakening. When I put it all together, there seemed to be a little more change going on than I was comfortable with. Feeling a little unsettled, I turned to my friend for reassurance.

"You have created for yourself a very comfortable substitute reality. Your greatest fear is that by making changes you will lose this comfortable life and it will be replaced by emptiness. You fear the unknown because the unknown represents emptiness. You believe that the Kingdom of Heaven is far away, therefore, it is an unknown, and this you fear. You believe that the Kingdom of Heaven is a big dark emptiness in which there is nothing, in which *you* are nothing. These are some of the beliefs that you will need to relinquish; only, you are as yet unaware of how simple and natural is the relinquishing of these foolish beliefs, for this is truly all that they are.

"When you were young, you learned that happiness was not a worthwhile goal in life. The teaching is not the issue. The issue is that you chose to accept that teaching—you chose not to be joyful. To not be happy is a goal that can only be set by a mind hell-bent on teaching the opposite of the truth of who you are as a child of God. God wants you to be happy now. If you are not happy now, it is because now you choose not to be happy.

"You accepted that teaching in your youth because it suited the goal of your teacher at the time—the ego, or your wrong mind. You did not question it, and you lived with it for many years—we might say now for far too many years. If you are not one hundred percent joyful, it is not because somebody taught you that being joyful was not an acceptable life goal, it is because you decided to accept that joy was not an acceptable life goal."

How true! I thought. Here I was, approaching sixty, wondering if it might be okay to look forward to enjoying life in my condo, without guilt, without obligation, for no good reason other than I just wanted to enjoy my life. After so many years asleep, the joyous child in me was beginning to stir and it felt good. But, the capable, cautious, responsible adult in me—read, ego—would need a little help to let go of the reins.

New Beginning

When that which is no longer needed comes to an end and is released, as often occurs in a 9 year, a period of integration follows during which relevant past experience comes together to form a new, cohesive whole. In that 9 year, on the verge of my second Saturn return, a point that would mark the start of a new thirty-year cycle, all the seemingly incongruous, broken and disconnected bits and pieces of my life began to rise to the surface. To my surprise, it appeared that I was in many ways returning to the starting point of the journey of this life. Why had it been necessary to go through all that senseless searching only to return to the very same starting point? Had it really been necessary? I knew it wasn't something God had wanted for me. Why had I experienced this long, drawn-out, circuitous journey? My friend helped me see more clearly on these issues.

"If you look back over your life, it becomes quite clear that the journey of this dream has indeed come full circle. When you were young, you were taught the simple truth. Most religions, in fact, most spiritual teachings begin with the same, simple premise: there is God, Mother/Father, a Source or an Eternal Life Principle whose primary quality or substance is unending love. This Source extends Itself, giving rise to Creation, which is like Itself, whole, eternal, united and loved.

"Like many of your brothers and sisters, you decided to take a little timeout from your state of perfect wholeness so that you could explore the possibility of being independent from your Source. This is, of course, something that was, and always will be, an impossibility, since perfect Oneness would not be perfect if even the least of Its expressions could separate from It. But, no matter; children will be children, and so you joined your brothers and sisters who were willing to play this game a while and engaged in a very believable round of make-believe, a game of 'let's pretend we are in our own world outside of Heaven.' Being imaginative as children of God can be, your pretend existence outside of Heaven, with all of its enthralling rules and laws, seemed so very real and exciting that you forgot that the whole thing was made up in the first place.

"After a while, being separate from your Source could only become uncomfortable, something you felt very early in life and that you experienced as loneliness, isolation and abandonment. You then set out to dampen those feelings by becoming busy in the world. The busier you became, the less you were bothered by your feelings of separation. In your teens, the pain of separation not quite alleviated, you searched for metaphysical, spiritual, psychological and even dietary causes of your unhappiness. *Divine discontent*, you called it—not without a little fondness, I might add.

"Having completely lost touch with the truth of who you are, long disconnected from your Father, you extended your search for contentment into the world of family, career and the general business of making a comfortable situation out of a makeshift world. Not once during those many years of searching did you look inside for the answer. Never entirely giving up, you eventually heard the call of *A Course in Miracles*, a work designed to turn your attention inward. Despite tremendous resistance, you persisted with this course of study—pun intended—only to discover that the truth has never changed. God is, pure and simple.

"Had you stayed with this one thought—God is—and wondered, *What is God Being here? What is God Being there? What is God Being in my brother? In my sister?*, you would not have needed this convoluted process of undoing. Everything else that you studied and learned served to make the thought of separation very believable and very real. Your self-imposed search for the truth implied that the truth had disappeared. You forgot that the truth cannot be altered, destroyed or taken from you. It has been right here all along. Now that you have come full circle, you no longer have need of this learning. The only thought that matters is the thought of God, and the learning you need will come as a natural expression of what God is Being in the moment."

Heaven is here and Heaven is your home. (*Song of Prayer*)

The Elephant in the Chapel

I understood that if being in a dream is not our natural condition, then awakening to our true condition must be normal and natural. To cling to the dream condition is not normal or natural. What is not natural can only be difficult, uncomfortable and contrary, hence the sense of struggle and challenge. Awakening then must be simple, maybe even easy, while sleeping is not natural, or very sane, for that matter. This much I knew, at least in theory. Yet, it still seemed like something that would not be coming my way any time soon.

For months, I pondered the subject of enlightenment, the state of awakening to our true condition of Being in the Kingdom of Heaven. In fact, it had become a daily pondering. In the past, I might have described it as another of my obsessions, but since it was a very peaceful thinking process and, in fact, could not be entertained if I was anything less than completely peaceful, I would have to describe it more as a subject of contemplation. What kept me focused is how the Course makes it all so approachable, so reasonable and so attainable. It teaches that Heaven is within reach, right here, right now, for everyone and anyone who so desires to experience it. It is not, as I had long believed, the distant and lofty state reserved for a select few, holy, deserving and very often, long-suffering Souls. In fact, all that is required for its attainment is a willingness to forgive, that is, to look over and beyond a world rendered by the limitations of perception, and to see that, in truth, Heaven has always been here, it has never changed nor has it been pulled from our reach. How could it be changed or taken away from us who are God's children? If that were at all possible, it would mean that either there is something that is more powerful than God or that God is cruel. Since God is love, it can only be that Heaven has never changed; it must therefore be that the way I see is what has changed. If I no longer see Heaven and Heaven is all there is, what I see must be an illusion, a fantasy. I must then heal the way I see.

During those moments of musing, one question occasionally—okay, make that frequently—came to mind. How long would it be before I could bridge what still seemed like a huge gap between the state in which I mistakenly believed myself to reside and my true state as God created me, as spirit, aware of our Being in Heaven? When I dared allow myself to formulate the words, it boiled down to this: How long will it take for me to wake up? Clearly, the question was founded within the framework of an illusory world, since in Heaven, there is no time, and thus this question had no real foundation. Yet, there it was, implying and reinforcing the idea—actually, nothing more than a lie—that something had happened, that I had left my worthy home and that there was someplace other than the Kingdom of Heaven.

I was on my way to the service station for a springtime tire and oil change. On a quiet stretch of road, heading against morning traffic, I pondered enlightenment once again. It should be within reach, since it is our natural condition. What was it then that still kept me from experiencing the fullness of my Being as God created me? Why would I not experience awakening right here, right now? The answer came swiftly, catching me off guard.

Women don't become enlightened!

Oh my God! There it was again—that tired old refrain that had troubled me in my youth. Jesus, Ramana, Thomas Merton, Yogananda… the long list of holy people—men—who had been my teachers throughout a lifetime of searching was proof that women were simply not candidates for holiness, let alone enlightenment. Women were meant to suffer, serve and wash feet. They even starve themselves into a state of socially acceptable littleness, remaining as powerless and inconspicuous as possible. This is not to say that there are no enlightened women in the world. However, this is the perspective that my increasingly nervous ego-identified self chose to entertain. Since my physical expression is female, and it is something I cannot change, it remained a handy target for attack. *Nice try, buddy,* I replied to the insane voice in my mind.

Instead of getting upset with myself for harbouring such regressive and clearly unenlightened thinking, I laughed. The old refrain was still there, a deeply buried belief, a lingering holdout, and there it was, momentarily blocking the way to my awakening. It was completely silly, yet it was something to which that part of me that believed in separation still clung. I retold this little bit of insight to a couple of friends and we laughed heartily, and as we laughed over the foolishness of the whole thing, another block of doubt and darkness dissolved, leaving peace, joy and hope in its wake.

Of course awakening has nothing to do with gender. I knew that. Nor had gender ever really kept me from pursuing my spiritual quest. Though it was not a belief I currently held, somehow it had nestled itself in the dusty trunk of my old beliefs. Now it simply needed to be looked at and released. From this experience I learned that the process of awakening need not be difficult, painful or uncomfortable; in fact, it could actually be fun and, as in this case, hilarious. There is no need to ferret out all of our blockages since they will naturally rise to the surface to be easily released when we are ready. To add to my revelations, my friend chimed in with a few additional insights.

"You still cling to the belief that enlightenment is for a select few special Souls. You still do not believe that it is for you, your family, your friends, your neighbours, everyone. You also seem to think that you are twenty to thirty percent up some imaginary ladder of spirituality. There is no ladder; there is no distance; there is no hierarchy of spiritual beings. That is a lie; it's a made-up story that says that there is a journey home. You are right now and at every single moment at the Gates of Heaven, at the threshold of awakening. There is no distance.

"Until you fully accept that you are worthy of the Kingdom of Heaven, you will believe there is a distance, there is a ways to go, years, months, none of which has ever been. You have simply chosen to look the other way and ignore the truth. The truth has not changed; it has never been altered. You are right now true at the threshold of awakening; all of you are right now at the threshold of awakening. This has always been so, and it will remain so until you accept the truth of your Reality in the Kingdom of Heaven. The return home is not a hierarchical climb or journey.

"In reality, there is no body; there is only mind. The experiences you appear to be having reflect what beliefs you have adopted. If you see yourself as body alone, this means that you have decided to forget the truth of what you are—mind. Male/female, yin/yang, these are dualistic principles that belong in a world of bodies. There is no male-female in reality. If you have identified yourself as either male or female, it is because you chose to identify with a frame of reference that is dualistic, or that reflects separation, multiplicity and division. You have chosen to adopt a thought system that is not reflective of Reality.

"All that is needed is that you acknowledge that you have made an error and simply be curious to see what Reality actually is. Be curious to experience the non-dualistic, all-inclusive nature of Reality. The idea that whether one appears to be in a male or female body has any validity or influence simply reflects the nature of the thought system you have adopted. This dualistic way of seeing reflects a decision to ignore the truth, the truth that says that there is One Thought expressed as many and that essentially all are the same."

The Disappearance of Misperception

How can I once and for all release any remaining deeply buried false beliefs about myself, especially the ones that are demeaning to the true nature of my Being? How can I let go of the past, my memories and my limiting beliefs about the world I see? What will happen to the world and my experience of myself in the world? My friend answered these questions, along with many others, while I was out for my daily walks.

"The world you see, the world you experience, exists in its current form only because, and as long as, you agree that this is so. A helpful step in releasing the past is to recognize why you cling to it in the first place. If you cling to the past, it is because it serves a purpose. Everything you choose serves a purpose; it serves either the Holy Spirit's purpose or the ego's purpose. If your decision leads to an experience of peacefulness and kindness, it is because you have chosen peace and kindness and you have chosen with the Holy Spirit. If what you have chosen leads you to feel unsettled in any way, it is because you have chosen to not be at peace, to be unsettled. Obviously, this means that you have chosen with the ego.

"You believe that once you awaken you will simply disappear and cease to exist, that there will be nothing left to experience. You believe that everything that you see will disappear. That is not true. When you awaken, you will simply cease to experience the world around you in a limited form. You will experience fully the meaning of everything that is there, all of what God is Being. How can everything disappear? What God has created cannot disappear. All that can disappear is your misperception, your made-up, incorrect version of what God created. When that disappears, then you see what God created in its full beauty and glory and breadth and scope. That is your natural way of experiencing what God is Being. You no longer see matter as a limited unmoving form. You see it change as God is Being it, as it is being made new every moment."

You have said many times that the physical or tangible expression of what is created will not disappear, but I still don't understand. What does that really mean?

"What it means is that from your awakened perspective that is not limited to the information transmitted by the organs of perception of the body and the ready-made interpretations that you, as a separated daughter of God, have made up for what these perceptions are, you will be able to see the natural moving, unfolding, changing expression and form of what God is Being right here, right now. Since God is Being that which is Being now without the limitations of memory and history, what God is Being is constantly new. So your experience of form and matter is constantly being renewed according to what God is Being in the moment. It is not something that you can control, remember, expect or foresee in any way. The physical expression is a very small part of the experience of what God is Being; nonetheless, it is part of the greater experience, which is love, light, perfection and life. So how you perceive matter and form will change because it will no longer be restricted by your current limited perception or by your definitions of what things are."

I had some misunderstandings about God's role in this world. As it says in the Course, God has nothing to do with the world, yet throughout the Course, we are invited to remember God. How can it be that God does not have anything to do with the world but then we are asked to rest in God, or told that God is the air that we breathe? Is He here, or is He not here?

"God does not have anything to do with the world as you perceive it, as you see it. You made up an illusory, fantasy version of what God has created. In order to see what God has created—because God *has* created the universe, only not the universe as you perceive it—you need to be willing to stop seeing your own version, your twisted and broken and dark version of what it is that God created. God did not create the world you see. God created a world, the universe, a creation that is perfect and whole. It is your perception of the world that needs correcting—your limited perception of a world in which everything is limited by form, a style of perception that precludes or prevents the full experience of the Oneness of All that God is Being in the moment."

"You exist in the middle of the Kingdom of Heaven, but you live as though there is an electric fence delimiting your own field of experience. You believe that you do not have access to the fullness of the Kingdom of Heaven, which is love. When you get close to that electric fence, you believe you will get a shock. However, the truth is that when you get close to that electric fence, those times when you come close to the edge of your limiting self-imposed boundary, are the times when you can actually look at it, go through it, and know that it is not real, that it has no power. *There is no force that can prevent you from the full experience of who you are as God created you.* You only believe that there is danger, that there is pain, that there is suffering beyond an imaginary fence that you have erected around yourself."

The message was finally beginning to sink in. Since God is the Eternal Source of life, God is Being right here, right now, and God is going to *be* regardless of whether or not I allow God to be. I may be very good at substituting my own version of reality but that does not change what God is Being in Reality. What God is Being is loving, whole and eternal. My goal became much clearer: to experience Reality. The first step in experiencing the wholeness of what God is Being now was to abandon my personalized version of what I perceived. What I wanted was the unedited script. What was going on in my house, my backyard, my life was *Life*, in its full beauty and joy.

Giving Up Control

As I continued to sift through my dwindling worldly possessions, I couldn't help feeling a little lost, as though I was going to lose something of value. Sometimes, I felt as though I had already lost something. The world didn't have the appeal that it once had; it felt too real for my comfort. I wasn't comfortable with the idea of being more deeply integrated into the world and this move business was dragging me further into the world.

"You fear that you are losing something and in part this is true. You are losing your limited perception. This is being gradually replaced by a broader vision of what is really there. What you are losing is ignorance; what you are gaining is knowledge."

I took this as an indication of progress of sorts, though it certainly did not feel that way. I had to admit that despite all this undoing, I felt stuck, going nowhere, with no purpose in life, and at the top of my list of things that were going nowhere was my writing, which had come to a dead halt.

"You are not stuck, as you believe yourself to be; you are simply temporarily disoriented. As you are practising leaning into what the Father is Being, you are relinquishing your habitual long-held practices of control, planning and deciding in advance what you will do and how you will do it. This book will get written with my help. You are simply at the moment temporarily lacking in confidence in me. This will soon change. You have already placed much trust in me and in this process of awakening. You have understood that this is not something that you will accomplish of your own will through study or through intellectual understanding. You now understand that the intellectual understanding was necessary in order for you to abandon intellectual understanding. Awakening is not an intellectual process. It is a process of relinquishing the intellect and controls and thinking."

In May, I was informed of a new delivery date for the condo. I would have to spend another entire winter at the house, with a move-in date as far away as the end of April 2013. I had to admit that my heart sank when I heard this news. I had begun to imagine myself spending Christmas at the condo, with indoor parking and no need to shovel snow.

"You have made a dream world in which you are comfortable. You are familiar with how it works and can control many aspects of it. When you encounter situations in which you feel discomfort, that is when you are reaching the edge of your comfort zone. The discomfort comes from the fear of not being able to control what might happen if you did choose a different way. It also comes from lack of trust. When you trust and allow yourself to lean into the Father, when you trust what God has there for you instead of your own controlled experience, then the discomfort will disappear.

"To relinquish control and your habitual way of doing things allows you to be ready to allow the Movement of Being, to allow what God is Being in you, right now. Although this appears to you as a new experience, it is an experience of moving into what is normal and natural for you. It is not new at all."

New Friends and Neighbours

One day, feeling an undeniable twinge of sadness at seeing so many memories disappear from my surroundings, I decided to clear my head and go for a walk. I had gotten into the habit of visiting the condo project at least once a week just to see how it was coming along. It took months for the excavation to be completed. By August, the foundation was finally poured and the structural work began to show signs of life. Construction was moving very slowly and I wondered how in the world the condo would be ready by April. It hardly seemed possible. Then someone suggested that perhaps I was making a mistake by selling the house and moving to a condo, and again, I wondered if I had made the right decision.

This time I chose to walk around the neighbourhood in the opposite direction to my usual path. Passing by the church where I had first seen the sign for the condo project, I noticed a poster for a Brahms concert that might have appealed to me had I not been so preoccupied with the deconstruction of my life. More importantly, because I was walking along the street from a completely different angle, I had a straight-ahead view of a nameplate on the brick wall next to the wooden doors: "Mary, Queen of Peace." I was even more astounded when I noticed the sign on the lawn: "Jesus, Light of the World Parish." For sixteen years, I had resided in this parish without ever having paid attention to the church in my neighbour-hood, no doubt because of an underlying aversion I still harboured regarding all things Catholic. Being that an aversion, no matter how seemingly justified, is nothing less than a judgment, it was time to relinquish that too.

From what I had learned from the Raj materials, my perception of Mary and Jesus had shifted radically. They were definitely not the Mary and Jesus of my Catholic youth. Whereas I had seen Mary as a lesser figure, even insignificant, now I came to appreciate the full strength of her devotion and love to the awakening, not only of her son at the time, but to all of humanity. Their role today was as awakened brothers and sisters, our equals, who truly have our best interests—awakening and healing—at heart. As I let this new realization settle into my Being, doubts and uncertainty faded. My neighbour at the condo was Mary, and Jesus was there to light the way. How could I possibly doubt that my life was unfolding accord-ing to the Father's Will!

> Indeed, Mary is very busy on your behalf, as I am; not as personalities, but as the Presence of the Christ intent upon illuminating your Christhood. Because ultimately the point is for you to join us in full comprehension and embrace of who you Are. It is not appropriate for you to be groveling at our feet and feeling embarrassed at even approaching us, because you and I are absolutely identical. (Raj, 1992, Saint Davids, PA)

Chapter 7

Teaching and Learning

No learning is acquired by anyone unless he wants to learn it and believes in some way that he needs it. (ACIM.T.1)

Confessions of an ACIM Addict

I was never very fond of school, even at one point suspecting that I might have suffered from some form of learning disability, though, more likely, it was just lack of interest due to the irrelevance of the material being taught. Being a practical person, I found it difficult to muster up the motivation to learn something that could not be immediately applied. My mind would toggle between watching what was going on outside the large classroom windows and day-dreams of life beyond school. The only thing that got me through school was fear, which was not a very good motivator for stimulating an appreciation for learning. I was afraid that if I didn't do well, I'd have to stay behind, which turned out to be the biggest motivator of all. My main concern throughout the school years was to get through and get out. While I managed to blend in by following the rules and not attracting undue attention, deep inside, I was a mystical child—a free spirit trapped in a body and locked in a cage called Catholic school.

By some blessed twist of fate, it seems that I was hard-wired to focus on the task at hand and to persist, no matter the obstacles. This trait, which I carried into adulthood, served me well when I stepped into the school of life—a hands-on classroom much more to my liking. Any studying that I engaged in, which, as it turns out, has added up considerably over the years, was solely for the purposes of accomplishing a task that I had judged to be worthwhile.

My studying and learning covered everything from how to make healthy baby food for my daughters to how to design websites for my business. The only academic subject that I ever enjoyed was mathematics. Math was logical and straightforward; it always came to a neat, clean resolution and so it resonated with my linear-thinking mind. Naturally, when I first encountered *A Course in Miracles*, the aspect of this teaching that immediately appealed to me was its logic. It made sense that I would approach the big blue book in the same manner that I had undertaken every other important learning endeavour in my life. I plunged right in with persistence, total dedication and—since it concerned a subject that actually engaged my interest—great passion.

Given my love of logic, structure and orderliness, I gravitated toward the more intellectual and rational approaches to the Course. I delved into the myth of separation with its colourful cast of characters and worked very hard at developing a neat, clean and intellectual understanding of the "metaphysics" of the Course. Eventually I became adept at recognizing the ego's guilty projections and fear-driven expressions in myself and in others. I was very pleased with myself for having been able to get a handle on the complicated theory of the Course, which I laid out with great flair in *Leaving the Desert*.

Hello. My name is Pauline and I'm a former *Course in Miracles* addict.

The fact that I had grown so enamoured with my Course studies, along with the works of certain teachers—read: exclusive of others—should have been a clue that perhaps something was amiss in my classroom. Truth be told, for the first couple of years of working with the Course, I was a true-blue *Course-in-Miracles* thumper. Have you heard of *A Course in Miracles*? You have to read this book! The Course has all the answers you need! I had become the kind of person I generally avoided like the plague, one who thinks that her way is the only way. Though my desire to share my passion for the message of the Course was sincere, it missed the point of the teaching.

Sadly, my well-meaning, though misguided, enthusiasm caused me to lose two of my best friends and some of my clients. Fortunately, I came to see the error of my ways, but more importantly, I learned to respect where each person is on their journey, rarely mentioning the Course to clients, and hardly ever to friends and passing acquaintances. If they were meant to work with the Course, it would find them. That was clear. When clients asked about the Course, I was careful to address only their questions and not elaborate further. I reined in my enthusiasm and forgave myself for my earlier outbursts of unbridled exuberance.

Since the ego had been my study buddy from the moment I began to work with the Course, it is safe to say that it was from the perspective of a separated, ego-identified self that I had enjoyed my Course studies. The truth is that the ego cannot possibly like the Course because the Course is designed to lead to its undoing! If I was enjoying my studies, it was probably because the ego's survival was not overly threatened. Studying the Course with logic, reason, analysis, intellect and, above all, independently of guidance had served to protect the survival of the separated self. Several years into my studies, I had become stuck on a comfortable "journey to awakening," awakening being little more than a vague mysterious transition that would lead to my ultimate disappearance into an equally vague indefinable place called the Heart of God. Bottom line, there was nothing to be concerned about, since I was not even a viable candidate for the position of awakened one.

No matter how logical, structured and lovely my analysis appeared, it remained an attempt at making something insane—the illusion of separation from perfect Oneness—into something logical, structured and orderly. Despite having become very attached to my new learning about the world and all things illusory, it was inevitable that, at some point, it would fall apart—and it did. I would eventually have to start turning my attention inward, to the uncovering of Reality. Fortunately, as described in *Choosing the Miracle*, that is what happened when I was guided to the teaching of Raj. While this new direction led to increased experiences of revelation and a strengthening of my conviction that I was finally on the right path, it was far less comfortable for the ego. Feeling seriously threatened, it stepped up its vigilance and attempts at sabotaging my efforts and weakening my resolve by using whatever means it could find. Its favourite areas of focus included my work with the Course, writing and my new partnership with guidance.

In search of further information about my never-ending quest, I turned, once again, to the Internet. It wasn't long before I became aware of some diverging, even contradictory approaches to the Course; evidently, not all teachers understood or taught its message in the same way. There was much talk and teaching around the Course, while there appeared to be significant gaps in its understanding. This led me to question the validity of the teaching approaches I had followed so faithfully for several years. How could I have been so naive! Peace of mind waned and confusion clouded my thinking. A part of me—guess which?—was looking to find fault with my learning, my work and whatever else it could snag along the way.

Given my newly shifting understanding, I started to feel guilty over the work I had done with the Course, in particular, my writing. Furthermore, my Internet findings had caused me to grow increasingly uncomfortable with all things ACIM. Since this was such an important aspect of my life, the struggle, the guilt and the doubts ran deep. Over a period of several months, as questions arose, I was blessed with the help I needed to release myself from the grip of these ego manoeuvres designed to keep me drowning in my feelings of guilt and self-doubt. Many of these answers have been gathered in the sections that follow.

Your Real Teacher

"You can assume that, once you have started on your journey with the Course, the ego is onto you. This condition will persist until you decide to take the journey with a different teacher, until you have consciously requested guidance. Most likely, at least in the beginning, your teacher, or your travel partner, is the ego. The ego's motives are really quite basic—survival at all costs. In order to ensure its survival, it will get involved in whatever it is that you are giving your attention to. While you have your attention on something, while you are preoccupied with something in the world, the ego's position as navigator of this journey is ensured.

"You can also assume that as you step up your desire to awaken, as you proceed on your journey inward, the ego will be equal to the task, even stepping up further, since its own survival is at stake. The only thing you need to keep in mind is that its survival is not in *your* best interests, and your awakening is not in *its* best interests. Where you focus your attention will determine where you will go on your journey.

"To seek out a teacher outside yourself is simply an indication of temporary lack of confidence in your own Inner Teacher. You will seek out a teacher who will confirm to you what you choose to believe at the moment. You will not seek out a teacher that will bring you beyond that which you are ready to accept at the moment. This will be so until you give up your desire to be the boss of what you believe or to be the determiner of your beliefs, until you reach a point where you give up this authority and say, 'I really don't know anything.' Then you will be in an open position, open to receiving teaching, open to learning something that will move you closer to the truth. Your next learning will always be in accordance with your current comfort level.

"In the end, you are your own teacher. You attract those lessons and those circumstances through which you can learn what you have chosen to learn. You will learn what the ego wants you to learn or you will learn what the Holy Spirit wants you to learn. Do not fuss or worry about who is teaching what kind of spirituality. Be concerned solely with how you feel about what you are learning.

"The Holy Spirit will bring to you what you truly need to learn. Your only true Teacher is inside you. It is either the ego or the Holy Spirit. The ego will teach you to remain in conflict; it will try to convince you that separation is valuable, that being separate, in a body, in the world, has something of value. The Holy Spirit will bring you to question this and gradually bring you to turn around, look inside your mind and ask for help. And, gradually, you will follow this journey Home to awakening.

"The Holy Spirit will be your Teacher on your journey to awakening. Since the Holy Spirit *is* your Right Mind, in the end you are your own best teacher; you have always been your only teacher. If you have attracted teachings that have confused you or kept you in the dark, that is because you have chosen the teacher of confusion and darkness. If you have encountered teachings that have brought you closer to the light, that is because you have listened to the call for light inside of you. In either case, your teacher has come from within you, never from without. How you experience external circumstances, teachings and situations comes from your decision to learn a particular lesson.

"There are only two teachings: the teaching of darkness, scarcity, loss, death, hatred, fear, anger, pain, sickness and suffering or the teaching of Eternal Life, Love, Beauty and the Glory of God. You remain always the one who decides which teaching you will pursue."

Spiritual Learning

"Theoretical or intellectual understanding, or the understanding of metaphysics, can be an important part of the process for an intellectual person. However, intellectual understanding alone will not take you home. At best, it will take you to the point where you realize that independent thinking must be abandoned.

"It's one thing to have an intellectual understanding of what the Course is teaching. This gives a basic understanding of the truth. However, in order to be lived, you must go beyond the intellect. The truth is known, and it is known through *feeling*. It is not reached through analysis; it is not understood in the way that you understand how things work in the world. The truth is known through an experience of *Being*, and there is only Being what God is expressing.

"You will learn only what you want to learn. In fact, you are not really learning at all. What you are doing is confirming or validating what you want to be true. So, whatever you believe you are learning, you are not learning, really. You choose what you want to learn based on which belief about yourself you wish to validate. The nature of the teachings you accept attests to what you want to believe, either that you are a separate individual or that you are one with God and have never left the Kingdom of Heaven—that which is Eternal. Remember that you remain always your only teacher, and that will simplify matters for you.

"There is no learning that is really required. The learning that you practise in your sleeping state is practised in order for you to reinforce your illegitimate, unnatural thought system of separation. In order for something unnatural to be sustained, it needs to be constantly reinforced. This is what you do in your learning situations. The Truth does not need to be learned, it is there waiting to be acknowledged. It has never been altered, nor can it ever be altered. Therefore, it is quite simple. All that is required is that it be accepted. It need not be learned because it is already there in you; it is part of you.

"What you call studying and learning, your spiritual quest, if you like, serves more as a buffer allowing you to move gradually, at a comfortable pace toward the Truth. This is because you are not entirely convinced at this time that you want the Truth. You still cling to the illusion that it is possible to have a life apart from your Father, so the learning allows you to move at a comfortable pace toward the Truth.

"The learning you experienced in the past several years through your work with the Course was needed in order that you might reach the point where you would be willing to question all that learning. In an awakened state, learning is not necessary.

"Intellectual understanding can only take you to the point where you realize that the only way to move forward is to abandon intellectual understanding. Experience, which leads to knowing, is not an intellectual event. Love is not an intellectual experience. Love is an experience of Being. Being is not an intellectual event. Intellectual activities are not natural. They are of the ego. Being is natural. The experience of Love, which is your natural condition, is natural.

"You cannot be a student forever, especially when the studying implies the absence of knowledge, a lack that needs to be filled with the information derived from these studies. The truth is that you are whole and the knowing awaits your experience. The knowing does not need to be learned through study. It needs to be allowed. What needs to be learned is that study needs to be relinquished. That is its sole purpose—to teach you that you do not need to be taught. The learning of the world does not have anything to do with the knowing of the Truth that is in you.

"You will only consider a teaching that you are ready to accept at the present time. If you are clinging to a teaching that is untrue, it is because you are fearful of the Truth. Again, the student must respect his or her current level of readiness for the Truth. This level of readiness is determined by the amount of fear that is still present. By trusting more and more in what the Father is Being, or by having more faith in the Holy Spirit or your guide, you will have more facility growing closer to the Truth. The fear will dissipate. Acceptance will grow. Revelation will occur. Revelation cannot occur as a result of intellectual deduction. Revelation is a gift. It occurs when intellectual deduction is relinquished.

"For someone who is fully steeped in illusions or lies, the Truth must be approached slowly, otherwise, great fear will be stirred up and progress, or awakening, will be further delayed. Since it is fear that breeds darkness in the first place, to increase fear would not serve purpose.

"The learning of the world can be seen as an amusement of sorts for as long as it serves your seeming function in the world. You can always rest in the confidence that all you need to know is there and waiting to be revealed to you. That which you need to know is not gained by study. That which you need to know is known simply by allowing, by setting aside your belief that something needs to be learned, by trusting that knowing cannot help but be known by its very nature. It cannot be changed or modified. It is in allowing yourself to *be* what God is Being in you that you will know what God is Being in you. Again, it is not the result of a lengthy process of study; it is an allowing."

How Can I Reconcile Conflicting Teachings?

When *Choosing the Miracle* was released, because of the shift in approach it introduced, some readers commented that they thought I had abandoned the Course altogether. There were important differences between Course interpretations and teachings, some of which were evidenced by open rivalry among its teachers. One thing that surprised me the most was the lack of interest in, even disregard for, the work of Paul Tuttle and Raj. Here was Raj/Jesus explaining his Course; it seemed only natural to defer to his wisdom on the subject. I stopped presenting myself as a *Course in Miracles* teacher or author, even going as far as saying, only half-jokingly, that I was a *Course in Miracles* graduate rather than a *Course in Miracles* student, and certainly not a teacher. This situation caused me to feel uncomfortably stuck, so I asked for guidance.

"Once again, here is an example of the ego using your current field of activity to serve its purpose of creating noise and confusion in order to obscure the truth. The truth remains that everyone is waking up, because, in truth, everyone is whole, born of love, spirit, created by God. Being asleep or ignorant is not a natural condition. Waking up is natural. That is the only thing that needs to be taken into consideration when looking at any situation. To look at the differences, or the mess that appears to be occurring in the process of awakening, is simply to cater to one of the ego's distractions. Do not pay attention to it. Awakening is a "wholeizing" and unifying process. To see differences, separation and hierarchies is a dividing process; it does not contribute to awakening and is a practice that should be abandoned. Awakening is not the result of following a structured or rigid agenda, curriculum or timeline. It is a natural process, a lot more fluid and flexible than most spiritual seekers believe it to be.

"Each person is teaching according to his or her current level of understanding, and that is normal. Each person, no matter his or her current level of understanding, has the ability to awaken at any given moment. There is no end point, no set goal or no measurable quantity of knowledge or understanding that is a requirement to awakening. There is only the willingness to uncover the truth.

"Because a person understands its message in a way that is different from the way you understand it, does not mean that it is inappropriate for them, or for any number of brothers and sisters. It only means that this is the way that the person understands it at the current moment. Again, because awakening is not a linear experience, there is no hierarchy of understanding. If you teach, write and share from the heart, from the centre of your Being, you will be an example of what the Course is teaching. This is all that is required of you. If you fear that you will be judged or attacked for your approach, it is only because you are projecting your own attack and judgment of other approaches onto others.

"If your Spirit has called you to write about, and teach, the message of the Course, then it behooves you to pursue this avenue with grace, equanimity and, above all, joy. Do not concern yourself with how other people are learning or understanding *A Course in Miracles*. Each person's awakening is already set into motion and ensured with absolute certainty by the fact that awakening is natural while ignorance is not. To see differences rather than to see global awakening is to choose to see with the dark lens of the ego, the lens of judgment. Awakening requires that you be willing to set aside the dark lens in favour of the Light of the truth of our wholeness in God. Because each individuality perceives in their own unique way, inevitably, each will experience their awakening in their own unique way.

"Even though awakening is an instantaneous event, many of you fear that you will disappear into the nothingness that the ego has told you is waiting for you should you awaken. This causes you to proceed 'with caution.' To have a variety of examples of brothers and sisters along the road to awakening can provide helpful signposts, even if they are signposts that read, 'Do not go down this road.' You do not object to a road sign that says STOP any more than you object to a green light. They are simply signs on the road. Similarly, some teachings will raise STOP signs for you, indicating that this is not the path for you, while others will give you the green light. It does not mean that once you have passed a green light that you will not encounter a red light or a STOP sign at the next corner. You simply abide by the signs along the road. You do not question them.

"The same with the guidance that is available to you on your journey of awakening. Abide by the signs that arise from within the centre of your *Being*. You will know which teaching is for you at the present moment. At the same time, be willing to accept that this teaching may not be suitable for you a year from now, a month from now or even a day from now. Ultimately, you are not the director of your awakening; it is your Spirit that guides you to your inevitable awakening. Your function is simply to accept what feels right for you today, at this moment, to not cling to it, and to accept what comes tomorrow.

"Similarly, the meaning of *A Course in Miracles* will be revealed to you according to your readiness to accept the truth. This is true of everyone who has accepted it as his or her path to awakening. Respect the integrity of their unfolding as you respect your own. Again, if you are called to share through writing or teaching, simply put your faith in your guidance, at the centre of your Being, and what you share or teach will be what is needed at the time that it is being shared. Do not be concerned that what you share or teach at a later date may be different. It is only natural that, as you become more and more aware of the fullness of your Being, more of your wholeness will be expressed in your sharing and teaching. To withhold your sharing and teaching is to withhold the natural expression of your Being. Again, trust that your Being has the wisdom to express Itself in a manner that is not only appropriate, but also kind, helpful and loving."

Ambushed by the Ego, Again!

Although I was grateful for the reassuring guidance, somehow there remained some uncertainty because I found myself avoiding *Course in Miracles* groups and activities, even going as far as removing some of the references to the Course on my website. Further guidance was not long in coming, and was clearly meant to remove any remaining ego tomfoolery from my mind.

"To want to separate yourself from *Course in Miracles* groups is simply another ego ploy for making you distinct and different from others. This is your typical ego pattern of separation. Give it up now. It serves no purpose other than to perpetuate differences, separation and differentiation. It is an ego game. You can and should, call yourself a *Course in Miracles* teacher and author because this is what you are; but keep an open mind and refrain from judging others. To do anything less is to play into the ego's game of judgment; it is not an example of true practice of the Course. Be one who practises what the Course teaches, which is, fundamentally, the withholding of judgment. This will lead to openness and acceptance, and the ability to see clearly what you want to teach and what you want to put on your website and what you want to share with others. Each person will be led to the approach that is suitable for him or her. And remember, don't take it so seriously. Have fun with your work and, in particular, with your writing."

Eventually, I came to understand that it wasn't the style or the method of teaching that had made me feel uncomfortable, but rather that it had worked—that it *was* working. The practice of the Course's teaching was leading to the ego's undoing, and this is what was uncomfortable. The lies were being revealed, the illusory structures were crumbling and I was experiencing the full discomfort of facing and removing the false definitions of myself that had been the foundation of my existence. The ego wanted someone or something to blame for this discomfort. The truth was that the discomfort I was experiencing was actually a growing awareness of the discomfort that is caused when we attempt to sustain a condition that is not natural, the condition of independence from our Source. Before proceeding with my work, I wanted to know if it was okay to put what I was learning into my own words, as I was doing in my writing.

"Do you believe that there are teachings outside your mind? What you perceive, what you learn is what confirms what you believe on the inside. Putting it into your own words helps you integrate it more directly and more comfortably in your own life. Why worry about the form of the teaching? Why focus so much on teachings that are outside of you or different from yours? If teachings that are different from yours cause you to reinforce differences and keep you in a state of conflict, then you know what it is that you are trying to learn: not a different teaching, but that there is reason to be defensive and that there are differences that do actually exist. They don't.

"A teaching that resonates with you does so only because you recognize in it what you are comfortable believing. A teaching that causes you to feel defensive, to attack a brother or to see differences is not about the teaching. It is about you wanting to be defensive and to feel vulnerable. It is you knowing on some level that you are clinging to a teaching but do not entirely believe it. It is an indication of your own inner conflict. In the end, it's not the teaching that matters; it's how it makes you feel. Do you feel at peace, or do you feel conflicted, angry, defensive or on the attack?"

Okay, message received. All my concerns had been addressed; well, most of them, for the time being, until new questions arose.

A Course in Miracles

"A Course in Miracles is a disturbing book, and it should be experienced as disturbing. It is not just a beautiful, literary work to be studied and admired. It is unsettling because it is designed to disrupt, or undo, all of your current belief structures that are currently founded on misperceptions, thus leaving you in a state of being face-to-face with the unknown. This can be frightening.

"The Course provides you with a practice. It acts as a bridge between your very limited experience of yourself in the darkness, or in the illusion, and the full experience of yourself in the light of Reality. The practice of forgiveness is part of that process of walking over the bridge to the truth. Looking for the more that is there is also part of the process. When awakened, there is no more need to look for the more that is there or to practise forgiveness.

"The study of A Course in Miracles is not about learning or acquiring a fancy new metaphysics. The metaphysics of the Course is there to act simply as a frame of reference for those who require a metaphysical conviction or convincing that there is another way.

"The Course addresses you, the student, at your current level of understanding, but also at your current level of readiness. It cannot induce you to do something for which you are not ready. If you are not ready to embark on one of its steps, you will simply disregard it, fall asleep or say, 'I don't understand this,' and leave it for later. When you are ready for a particular step in your learning, it comes easily and is effortless. You simply integrate it into your current level of knowledge, and then your current level of knowledge—your knowingness—expands.

"You cannot learn something that you are not ready for, nor can you be harmed by a learning that you are not ready for. Your defence mechanisms will protect you. These are not evil defence mechanisms or ego resistances. This is your Divine Self that knows, from your divine inner wisdom where you are and what you are capable of assimilating. It is wisdom, not resistance. You cannot force awakening onto yourself any more than you can force it upon another. It occurs when you are ready. It is pointless to put yourself down or belittle yourself for your lack of readiness. On the contrary, praise yourself for having gotten as far as you have, and keep moving forward. Don't look back, look at the road ahead.

"The purpose of a good spiritual teaching is to lead the individual to that point of recognition of his or her wholeness. It is not to build a broad base of practitioners, students or followers. The goal of spiritual study is not to become well versed in a teaching or an expert in 'the field.' The goal is to lead to a shift in perception.

"When comparing spiritual teachings, ask yourself what it is that you truly want. Do you want to find a teaching that works for *you*, or do you want to claim some form of authority by declaring that you have determined which is the best teaching of all, for all? In the end, the best teaching is the one that brings you one step closer to the truth of your wholeness, or your *holiness*. It is the teaching that brings you closer to accepting the Father's Will. One teaching may be suitable for you at one point in your life and then later no longer be suitable. There cannot be only one teaching, or only one way of interpreting a teaching. The best one is the one that works for you *now*.

"The point of studying is not to amass vast quantities of spiritual or metaphysical data or concepts. The point is to ask for help, and if it comes in the way of a book, take that which you need to move further toward your awakening, that which you need that makes you feel comfortable and not overly threatened, and then move on."

How to Choose a Path

What is the best path to follow if one wants to awaken from the dream? How do we know when it is time to change paths?

"The best path to follow is the one that comes to you when you have sincerely and peacefully requested a path. Ask, Father, what is the best way Home? You will know it is time to change paths when you simply and calmly realize that it is time to change paths. There will be no debates, intellectual arguments or endless analysis; it will be a peaceful shift. You will know, now is the time for me to move on to this new path. This will be the quickest and simplest way to move forward on your journey Home. Should you encounter conflict, confusion or doubt as to whether a path is the right one for you, you could be facing the ego's resistance. The ego will not appreciate your engaging in a spiritual pursuit of any kind. Simply do not give it any attention. Find peace. It is in a peaceful state of mind that you will know what needs to be done.

"It is also possible that at a particular crossroads, or a particular transition period of your journey in the dream, there is no path to follow. Sometimes, the absence of a path is the path, and it may be the most productive, rewarding path to follow at that time. Again, you will know what to do when you are quiet and receptive to hearing guidance.

"There is no perfect path; there is no single path that suits everyone. Paths are also of the dream. The perfect path is the one that works for you now. There is only the acceptance of the Truth. God is. That is the shortest path. Though that may be the shortest and simplest path, it is certainly not the path that is the favourite of those who believe that God is but there is also this, and there is that and hundreds of other things in between. In the end, the seeker will realize that there is no path because there is no distance. You are in, and have never left, the Kingdom of Heaven, and so there is nowhere to go on this path. The path acts as a buffer, if you like, making the return Home as gentle and as comfortable as possible for those who still see themselves as separated sons and daughters of God, for those who still identify with the ego.

"There is no hierarchy of spiritual teachings. There is the teaching that you have chosen to validate your current point of view, which, at the same time, also reflects your personal limit of comfort. At some point, you will have to get your head out of the book and your heart out into the world.

"The Course uses your beloved intellect to almost tease and bring you to the point where you realize that your intellect is actually going to be in the way of your goal of awakening. You must be brought to that point delicately especially if you cling dearly to your intellect.

"Remember also that you cannot awaken by following in someone else's footsteps. You must retrace your own footsteps. By that, it does not mean that you have to go back over every single event of your life. However, you must acknowledge the beliefs that you have set in place, the beliefs that allow you to think, or that lead you to think, that you are anything but a child of God forever residing in the Kingdom of Heaven. This is your way to awakening. It is not someone else's. Take from other people's experiences those teachings that appeal to you; take only what will help you retrace *your* steps back Home. That is the fastest way for you to awaken.

"A teaching is only as good as its resulting learning. A teaching that begins with the intellect should end with learning in the heart. A teaching that remains in the intellect has gone nowhere."

The End of Learning

It became clear to me that the learning we engage in serves to strengthen the beliefs we have adopted. More than that, it was a relief to know that learning is not necessary at all since, as God's Expressions, we are whole and not lacking for anything. Since God is the Author of us, then all we need is to allow for what God is Being to flow through us and we will experience and learn through the very simple act of Being. Teachings serve as a bridge to take us a little bit closer to the truth. They are there to facilitate unlearning and the removal of the learning that has kept us from the truth. In the end, it doesn't really matter what spirituality a person practises, or even if they are following a spiritual teaching at all. If you really want to know what God is Being and you do not have an intellectual cell in your brain, it is possible to discover the truth by simply sitting in the garden and asking, what is God Being in the flowers? In the bees? In the grass and in the trees?

"You might call it not so much the end of learning, but the end of active studying, with the emphasis on *active*. As long as you are actively doing something from your limited, separated point of view, there is no allowing. Now the true learning—the allowing—can happen. The kind of learning that you have committed to is a gentle, enjoyable learning. It will lead to a joyful uncovering of the truth that is there. It is not a frightening or stressful occurrence.

"All teachings fall within an ego framework. The only true teaching that occurs comes from the Father. True learning is the gift you receive when you allow yourself to flow with the Father's Will."

Tips for Teaching, Studying and Learning

What are the criteria for identifying a good path? How can we distinguish a good path from an ego distraction? What is the best way to learn?

- A good path will be simple and peaceful—not complicated.
- It will feel right and, most likely, will lead to an experience of the heart.
- It will inspire you to be kind and loving toward yourself as well as others, rather than judgmental and fanatical.
- It will not push you to do things that are in conflict with your integrity.
- Because a teacher speaks with great authority, it does not necessarily mean that he or she speaks the truth.
- A good path will be all-inclusive. It is not selective; it is not hierarchical.
- A good teaching does not judge others nor condemn other paths.
- You will feel respected at your current level of knowledge and understanding.
- If you feel in any way demeaned or belittled, or urged to go in a direction that is uncomfortable, it is likely an ego path.
- You will feel safe and supported.
- It's never about the form of the teaching; it's always about what you want to ascertain.
- There are no right or wrong teachings; there is only what you want to learn at any given moment.
- If some part of a teaching does not sit well with you, don't feel obligated to accept it, no matter who the teacher is.
- Remember to let yourself be guided from within.

- Because a path is suitable for your partner, the president, your family or your friends, it does not mean that it is the right path for you.

- Because a path is suitable for you, it does not automatically follow that it is the right path for others.

- The best way to learn is to give up being your own teacher. Yield to the Teacher within.

- By joining with the Holy Spirit, your learning will be more graceful, more enjoyable and certainly easier.

- If in doubt as to whether or not a path is right for you, leave it alone. If it is right, it will return again and again, until it feels right.

- Remember that each person has his or her own Teacher.

- The best way to teach the Good Word to others is in silence.

Chapter 8

Innocence Reclaimed

Innocence is strength, and nothing else is strong.
(ACIM.T.23)

Guilt: The Gift that Keeps on Giving

Everyone has done things for which they feel a little less than proud, most likely guilty, and perhaps even profoundly guilty. What do we do when thoughts of past actions come to mind and disrupt our peace? How can we handle the overwhelming guilt that is attached to mistakes, errors in judgment and bad decisions when the stain of memories rises to the surface and refuses to let us forget? Even if this is a dream, to us simple slumbering sleepers, these memories refer to our very own, very real experiences. What's more, we can likely point out any number of willing witnesses who will gladly attest to our guilty transgressions. We cannot change what we did in the past, nor can we erase the past. So, how do we deal with the memories? How do we release their hold on us? I asked my friend for help with these concerns and, once again, he was very generous with his answers.

"This is a very good question in that, not only is it filled with clear examples of convoluted and clever wrong-minded thinking, at the same time it shows the desire and the willingness to see things differently. As such, it holds the promise of resolution because the truth is always just on the other side of any question. The act of posing a question is an important step in the process of returning the mind to its natural state of wholeness because it opens you up to the possibility that there might be another way of seeing.

"A situation that appears to arise within the dream can never be properly addressed from within the dream, at least not if your goal is to attain a level of conscious awareness of your true state of being awake in Reality. If you wish to rise above a dream situation, you must look at it from outside the dream, away from the false structures of your ego beliefs, from within the framework of your Right Mind. Only then can it be looked at and recognized for what it is. Keep in mind always that the ego lies, so if you look for an answer within the dream, which is basically one huge lie, you will find more lies.

"To be able to look at a situation from outside the dream requires a conscious decision to see things differently and this can only be achieved from a centred, peaceful state. You will not see truth if you are preoccupied, anxious, upset or in any way distracted by what appears to be occurring in a world defined by limited perception. From within the dream, your ability to see is bound by that which is being perceived, and perception reflects what you have chosen to experience. If you are not at peace, you will see the many justifications for your lack of peace, because this is what you have chosen to experience. What you see justifies your choice.

"The first step in seeing things differently is always to consciously decide to re-establish peace. This can be achieved by a number of means such as meditation, yoga practice, a long soak in a hot bath, going for a walk or listening to soothing music. Use whatever method works for you. If you are not at peace, you will be looking from within the ego frame of reference and therefore you will not find a solution that reflects the truth. If you are not at peace, do not even think of how to resolve the situation, for you will not see the truth. First, seek peace.

"The next step is to ask for guidance. When thoughts of guilt over past actions arose, with whom did you look at the disturbing thoughts? Most likely it was by yourself, and a separated self is always guided by the ego. You are not likely to be successful in your attempts at seeing the situation differently on your own since independent thinking is usually at the source of the problem. Ask for help: Father, what is the truth here? Ask your guide: Help me see this situation truthfully. If you can allow yourself to have faith that you will be lovingly supported and guided, you will find almost immediate relief, making it easier to establish and maintain a state of peace.

"Recognize the problem for what it is. Once again, as with all troubling situations, thinking is the problem. Guilt is a thought. It arises as the result of your having accepted a belief that is nothing more than a lie. It does not matter what the apparent source of the guilt is, the thought of guilt is just another effective means of keeping you preoccupied within the dream. It is never about what you did or did not do. You feel bad because, by all appearances—that is, from your limited viewpoint—you have judged that you have done something wrong for which you should suffer some form of punishment. It is a judgment that you have made from your independent way of seeing things, from within the framework of a separated self.

"From within the dream, it does not occur to you that you did what you did while in a temporary state of ignorance, in a state of dreaming, and therefore not in your true state of Being in the fullness of who you are as God created you, therefore in a state that can have absolutely no effect in Reality. All you are aware of is your feelings of guilt. If you had looked at the situation with the loving presence of the Holy Spirit or your guide, or your Father, you might have seen it for what it was—the act of an unguided child believing that it is possible to function independently of the Father. Since nothing happens outside the Mind of God, whatever appears to happen only does so in your imagination and so cannot have any effects in reality. Whatever happens in the dream is never real.

"Additionally, the thought of guilt also serves the very important purpose of reinforcing your belief in your unworthiness as a Child of God. At the root of the thought of guilt is the belief that it is possible to achieve the impossible: to exist independently of your Source. If you are guilty, you are not worthy of God's Love. You are well aware by now that the study and practice of a spirituality such as *A Course in Miracles* is designed to turn your attention inward, toward the truth of your real Being in the Kingdom of Heaven, in Reality. It is only normal that your small sense of separated self would react in fear as you progress toward uncovering the truth about your true Self. As long as you believe that guilt is possible, the thought of guilt will continue to catch your attention. The ego-identified self, clinging to the last threads of its survival as a seemingly separated individual, will use this belief in guilt to its advantage.

"As you begin to fully grasp the truth that the sons and daughters of God are not guilty, have never been guilty nor could they ever *be* guilty by virtue of their Divine Source, guilt will cease to be an effective weapon of distraction. If you see guilt in a child of God, it is because you are indulging in your misperceptions. The truth is that guilt does not exist in the Kingdom of Heaven and nothing exists outside of the Kingdom of Heaven. If you perceive guilt, it is because you have momentarily chosen to replace the truth with a lie; you have chosen to misperceive.

"Memories too are thoughts. Everyone knows how unreliable memory is. No two people ever remember a situation with exactly the same perceptions and images. To base your feelings, your estimation of your worth or any evaluation of yourself on memories is to base your feelings on nothing. Memories should be your least reliable source of information for any situation. More than that, what God is Being is always new. To mull over, or to cling to—let alone feel guilty over—something that occurred in a dream is to prevent what is natural from occurring, what God is Being *now*.

"The past does not exist and it has no power; it only seems to have power when used inappropriately, by the wrong mind, to sustain memories of guilt. It does not have the power to heal; this exists in the present only where a real choice can be made. So, how do you deal with troubling thoughts of guilt that arise from memories? As you would do with any other troubling thoughts, you simply dismiss them. If you can't stop the thoughts, then find something else, something fun and enjoyable to occupy your thoughts, and just keep moving forward. Healing occurs now; you can only be here now by letting go of the past.

"If thoughts of the past make you feel guilty or uneasy or uncomfortable in any way it is because you have chosen to feel guilty or uneasy or uncomfortable. That is all there is to it. The past does not exist. To bring up the past and to feel uncomfortable is simply to use a convenient excuse for feeling uncomfortable. It is not because of something that may or may not have happened in the past. How you feel is the result of a decision you made beforehand. You decided to feel peaceful or you decided to feel not peaceful. Keep it simple. I said I would keep it simple for you. It does not get any simpler than this."

Heavenly Court

I was at the clinic seeking help for a urinary tract infection, the second bout in as many weeks. This time, I had brought a large canvas bag to carry water and reading material and to serve as a seat. If I was going to wait in line for nearly an hour before the clinic opened, it would be from a seated spot on the floor. Why had I brought this annoying condition on myself? It didn't take me long to identify the source of the problem, a conclusion that would soon be supported by the doctor.

In the process of downsizing and emptying my life of whatever I would not need in the condo, I had decided to purchase less expensive products for my cherished daily bubble baths. How a cheaper bath product would give me more space in the condo was a mystery; I just had this thing about finding the better deal. As it turned out, the new product upset my body's pH, hence the resulting condition. Although my usual bath products were not terribly expensive, I recognized that my decision came from a longstanding belief in my lack of worth and, of course, guilt. I was not deserving of the more expensive product. Come to think of it, I was not deserving of too much good, and whatever good I had in my life came with a hefty price tag: guilt. I thought about the problem of guilt and its persistent nature, and as I sat on the floor outside the clinic doors, I was urged to pick up my pencil and start writing. And so I did.

"Do not waste time analyzing the cause of your guilt. Do not give it any more life and power than it already has. What is important is to acknowledge that you are choosing to judge yourself as being guilty. It is a choice *you* are making. This is the only thing that you need to be concerned with at the moment. If in truth you are not guilty because guilt is an ego concept, then the truth is that you must be innocent. You are more comfortable with the thought—the belief—in your inherent guilt. This is what you are familiar with. It is guilt that was the driving force behind all of your decisions in the dream. Although you have read and learned that all of God's children are without guilt, hence innocent, it is a concept you have not yet accepted and embraced with respect to yourself. You are beginning to see guiltlessness in others when you work with them in consultation and as you go about your daily activities, but you have not as yet extended guiltlessness to yourself.

"The subject of your guilt is always a clever distraction that serves the purpose of keeping you from the truth, in this case, the truth of your innocence. You have not yet given yourself the opportunity to consider that you might be innocent too! Being accustomed to the feelings associated with this long-standing belief in your guilt, you have not yet fully experienced the feelings associated with your innocence, such as love, joy and peace. This is a new trio on your daily menu. Give yourself time for it to become your preferred choice. Become accustomed to the ramifications of this choice, such as the absence of fear, worry and concern for money, and so on.

"If all of God's children are innocent, then *you* must be innocent too! If you are not guilty, you must be innocent! Chew on this for a while. Wonder what it might feel like to know, with absolute certainty, that this is the truth. Desire to experience your innocence more than your guilt. For now, these are only words—nice words, you might say—but words nonetheless. Make your innocence a true experience *now*. Try it. I guarantee you that it will feel better than anything based on guilt can serve up. As long as you continue to believe in your guilt, as long as you continue to reject the truth of your innocence, you cannot, nor will not, fully accept all of the help and support that is the birthright of God's children. It will be difficult for you to accept healing, abundance and love."

Later that day, I was presented with what seemed like a goofy exercise, but by its goofy nature, it helped relieve some of the senseless seriousness associated with the subject of guilt.

"Do the following exercise when you feel overwhelmed by guilt, or when you suspect that guilt is behind your thoughts, which is likely whenever you are not at peace.

"Find a quiet spot and settle down as though in preparation for meditation. Allow the guilt-induced thoughts to rise to your awareness. Imagine a courtroom in the Kingdom of Heaven. It is brightly lit and decorated with large bouquets of freshly picked flowers. A jovial round-faced man with twinkling eyes and lips that have never formed a frown sits behind the desk and invites you to stand before him. There is no jury; there are no witnesses or attorneys; only you and the gentle judge."

In my mind, I imagined a very large man, lost in flowing white robes. He looked more like Santa Claus then an icon of the justice system. Goofy as it all seemed, I played along.

"He invites you now to present your case, in your own words, as simply as you can. Mentally express what you feel and believe to be your guilty act for which you think you need to be punished. Once done, simply wait for the judge's findings.

"The judge ponders your presentation a moment, and then declares, 'Not guilty!' Not guilty is the only verdict he can declare for that is the truth. This verdict is irrefutable. The one law of this court is that you must accept this judge's verdict.

"Not guilty!"

The sound of the gavel hitting the imaginary desk made me chuckle. My friend continued with his silly story.

"Repeat this as often as thoughts of guilt arise. This will help break the habit of assuming the existence of guilt.

"'Innocent!' The judge declares with love and great joy.

"Allow yourself to feel the profound relief, the joy and the light-heartedness of being officially declared innocent.

"Not guilty! The sons and daughters of God are all innocent."

Guilt-free Writing

While writing had become an integral part of my healing process, it was also a journey that I shared with readers, clients and fellow students. As mentioned, my ego-identified self did make very liberal use of my writing as a weapon for stirring up guilt. It even went so far as to attempt to convince me that, since I was really not a holy person, by virtue of my taking such a long time to awaken—and certainly not destined for enlightenment any time soon—I should remove all my Course-related books from the marketplace. And so it took a while before I felt confident enough to pick up my pen once again.

Fortunately, as with all things, there were really only two ways of looking at the situation: I could continue to use writing as a helpful tool for awakening or I could use it to stir up guilt, fear and doubt. Let's just say that I no longer felt the attraction of any other option besides awakening. Still, there was the small matter of lingering ego beliefs, and it seemed that the more awakening became a very real possibility, the more subtle and vicious were the ego's attempts at maintaining its stranglehold on my mind.

Eventually, I began preparing to write again. Summertime was approaching, business was slowing down, as was common at that time of year, and the garden would soon come into its full beauty. It was time to write. Still, I hesitated. A niggling spot of self-doubt prevented me from returning to my cherished writing, reciting a familiar refrain: The world did not need yet another book on *A Course in Miracles*, much less one from *me*. It was tempting to conclude that I should just leave well enough alone, move on to another form of activity, perhaps another career or maybe even get a job in a flower shop, although that option had already been removed from my list. This awakening business, I feared, was way beyond my spiritual aptitudes.

For weeks, I waffled in this haze of uncertainty, coming up with a variety of plausible justifications for not writing. I should take a break, three books was enough; there were better books out there. I even tried to convince myself that I no longer needed to bring my recorder when I went for my daily walks, those times when I felt closest to God and to guidance. It was obvious where that invitation had come from: no recorder, no opening up to guidance, no listening, no hearing, no learning and no getting closer to awakening. The ego is a clever devil!

However, I had been growing into the habit of becoming quiet; allowing myself to lean into the Father's Will. I was beginning to slowly—make that very, very slowly—relinquish my control over the events of my life, from the details of everyday activities to the larger, seemingly more important matters. From that quiet place of surrender, it became clear that part of my function in this life had always been to write, and to do so was simply to respect the integrity of who I am. From that quiet place of surrender, there came a tremendous feeling of safety and support. I knew that I would be guided. Although I knew this from the bottom of my heart, since this was a new way of looking, I was still frequently confronted with my habitual ways of dealing with situations big or small.

Despite the doubts and the old habits, I continued to grow aware of the presence of the one I had accepted as my friend. Of course, increasing awareness did not always remove the doubts I felt about my connection with Jesus. It was a gentle presence, unimposing and very patient; it would have to be, given that I was such a slow learner. Even though it had been a year since I had begun the practice of joining with guidance, given my lingering self-doubt, it was a presence I still kept at arm's length.

Nevertheless, I was determined to continue on this path. Now long past returning to ancient beliefs, the old way of looking held absolutely no place in my current view of the world and the universe. I felt, once again, as though I was in an in-between place of sorts; there was no fear, no urgent need of any kind, no burning desire. It was a relatively peaceful place, but I sensed that it was temporary. It was a bridge that would enable me to eventually find my bearings. Actually, in my new direction, my bearings would no longer be up to me. I took the hand of Jesus and expressed my concerns about my writing.

"You do not have to worry about becoming a "channeller" or about having the responsibility of scribing another major spiritual work such as *A Course in Miracles*. You are not a channeller, nor a scribe. What you are is a practising student of *A Course in Miracles*; let me correct that—a practising *graduate* of *A Course in Miracles*— and you are doing exactly what has been asked of its students. You are living your life and gradually shifting your allegiance from the ego as your teacher to the Holy Spirit, or your Right Mind, as your Teacher. This is what is asked of all students. This is possible for all students. You need not worry about how you are proceeding. Simply trust that you are doing what is needed for your present goal—your present goal having now shifted from success and survival in the world, to awakening to Reality. It is really that simple.

"You are writing because, first, you are a writer and, second, it serves purpose. Your sharing, as you call it, can be a helpful tool for showing not only how asking for guidance works, but also that asking leads to the actual receiving of guidance. You are not doing anything unusual or anything that any of your brothers and sisters cannot do themselves. You are, in fact, showing that this is how it is done; it is that simple. You don't have to be especially gifted to listen to the guidance that will take you Home. Each and every one of you can do this. Know that if your commitment is to awakening, you will have the help you need to reach that goal.

"Your concern is that you will be judged. Your concern stems from your pattern of thinking. You would have judged a brother or sister for listening to guidance from me, which is something you actually did in the past. You assume that others will judge you in the same way. If your brothers and sisters judge you for your writing, know that it is nothing personal; they would have judged you if you had been a seamstress or a truck driver. Know that if you are being judged by a brother, it is that he has not abandoned the practice of judgment and is thereby depriving himself of an experience of joining, the only experience with true meaning. Judgment is a problem for *him*, not *you*.

"If you are bothered or affected by a brother's judgment of you, it is because a part of you has decided to believe what has been said. By now, you can immediately recognize the ego's hand in this perception of a situation that has no bearing on Reality in the first place. Accepting a judgment as being true just reinforces your belief in your guilt. It simply means that you have been looking at the situation with the wrong teacher. Change teacher, now.

"I have said this before—the goal of the Course is not to become a good *Course in Miracles* student or teacher, for that matter. There is only one teacher of the Course, and that is the Holy Spirit, which is your Right Mind. The goal of the Course is to bring your awareness to that point where you can consciously make a choice for your true state as an awakened son or daughter of God. How each person approaches this teaching is unique to that person. How each one applies it in the practical day-to-day circumstances of their lives is simply a matter of individual choice.

"Though, in Reality, each one shares in the One Mind of God, each person's journey is unique; and so it only follows that each person's journey Home will be unique. Do not be concerned that some of your brothers and sisters might be uncomfortable with your journey; the discomfort they experience is a point of information for *them*, serving as a reflection of their own discomfort in the face of the truth with which they so desperately struggle. The only struggle you need to attend to is between your desire to experience the truth, and your desire to cling, just a little while longer, to the fantasy.

"Also, you do not need to write from the perspective of *A Course in Miracles*, or from the perspective of any other teaching, for that matter. Write from the perspective of what God is Being in *you*. That is the only concern that you should have. There is nothing else of value. Keep your attention on bringing forth what God is Being in *you*. From that perspective, you will experience what God is Being in your brothers and sisters."

Despite these very supportive words from Jesus, when I came to focus my attention on getting this book underway, I encountered continued resistance. I loved writing. Although I had no illusions about being a great writer, I had begun to consider myself to be a writer and I did have a book to write. But it seemed that every time

I set aside a day to work on the book, resistance arose in the form of various arm, neck and back pains. Darkness would cloud my thinking and I couldn't bring my heart into the writing. I struggled with this for weeks, and as the days passed, I realized that I was growing further and further away from the guidance that had become so near and dear. Doubt arose and, in particular, self-doubt.

There was only one thing to do, only one way to address the issue. Say no! The only way to return to the guidance and to the inspiration that guided my writing was to refuse the invitation to pay attention to anything else. As I walked that day, recorder in hand, I decided that I would not be delayed by doubt, or guilt or fear or any form of ego suggestion. I was going to be still and quiet and focused on the altar within, focused on hearing, sensing and knowing the truth. I was not turning back and I was not giving up.

As I went about the normal business of the day, any time that did not require my undivided attention was focused on this thought. I kept my mind free of cluttering thoughts and doubts and continued to pray for the clarity and guidance that I needed. I was going to get through this. My determination was total; it was far, far greater than any temporary resistance. In my meditation that evening I struggled with a lot of back and neck pain. But I didn't quit. This was not going to stop me. I still didn't hear any guidance as I went off to bed that evening. But I trusted that all the help I needed was around me. I fell asleep in the comfort of the love that surrounds all of us, regardless of the fact that I thought I was temporarily disconnected from it.

The following morning, my cat Maggie told me in her clear and commanding *meow* that it was time to get up. I squinted at the digital clock, eight o'clock. That was late for me. As I stretched and moved and prepared to get up, I realized that most of the pain in my body was absent. In a glimpse of guidance, it was made clear to me that much of the blockage and the physical pain had been due to guilt that I still clung to over things I had done in the past. I reminded myself that whatever I had done had come from the heart, that I had done my best in every situation in my life, as is the case with everyone else. We all do our best in the moment.

As clearly as I had heard Maggie's wake-up call, in a gentle, loving tone, I heard the following words, "This is my Daughter in whom I am well pleased." Yes, I thought, not for a second questioning the Source of the words. It was time to release the guilt, I concluded, as tears streamed down my face.

Chapter 9

On the Road to Awakening

As the light comes nearer you will rush to darkness, shrinking from the truth, sometimes retreating to the lesser forms of fear, and sometimes to stark terror. But you will advance, because your goal is the advance from fear to truth.... Truth has rushed to meet you since you called upon it. If you knew Who walks beside you on the way that you have chosen, fear would be impossible. (ACIM.T.18)

An Unwanted Invitation

You might think that with all of the wonderful guidance and support I had received over the past couple of years that I'd be pretty close to the end of my journey of awakening, maybe even at its end. There were moments when I actually thought that I could simply allow myself to be in the Presence of God and happily sail into the Kingdom of Heaven without any interference from my dark companion. Note that I said moments, because I knew very well that the ego wouldn't give up its cherished stronghold in the kingdom of my sleeping mind without a fight. The truth was that it was more likely to fight even harder as the light grew nearer. Well, fight it did. I had savoured glimpses of the love that awaits us when we allow ourselves to be in the Presence of God, and I wanted more—I wanted it all the time. And so it was that the ego found itself face to face with a formidable foe.

The fourth obstacle to peace, the Course points out, is the fear of God. Given my growing commitment to choosing peace and my burgeoning relationship with my Father, the ego would have to find new ways of generating fear. If it succeeded in distracting me with worldly fears, its true fear, the fear of God, would remain hidden. Its survival no longer a sure thing, it had no alternative but to step up its game. Since the ego's goal is to win at all costs, it tends to be an unfair player and so has no qualms about attacking us where we are at our weakest and most vulnerable. I call it the survival slut! Not being a terribly imaginative player, as usual, it turned its attention to whatever was important to me at the time.

With the issue of writing successfully squared away, the ego needed to come up with a new call to arms; it needed material to suck me into a new battle. It appeared that I was not about to sail smoothly into the light of awakening without at least a little turbulence along the way. It was not that resistance or turbulence, challenges or obstacles of any kind were a requirement to awakening, but rather that my dwindling allegiance to my dark companion drew them onto my path. If there were obstacles that appeared real, then there was a state of separation from my Source that appeared just as real. This was the only state in which the ego could exist.

All obstacles to peace would need to be released if I was to awaken to the fullness of my Being, including fear. I was learning first-hand that there is only one way to deal with fear, and that is to withdraw attention from it. This also turned out to be the quickest and simplest way to be rid of this highly resistant barrier to the truth. Since all the ego can do is put forth an invitation, we always remain free to ignore that invitation. It suggests that since you are vulnerable, you should take extra precautions, maybe even protect yourself against this upcoming dangerous situation. The only appropriate response to an unwanted invitation is *no*. And it doesn't even have to be a polite no. Say "no" as many times as the invitation arises, and since the ego knows how to use automatic reminders, this can happen many times. In fact, the ego will try to wear down its opponent with whatever might appear appropriate artillery in the face of a potential weakness.

Since forewarned is forearmed, I was more than adequately prepared when I received a call from a real estate agent who was most eager to share her assessment of my plan for selling the house. In the weeks prior to her call, I had thoroughly researched the subject, enough to make a decision with which I felt comfortable. After reviewing evaluations and proposals from a number of agents, I decided to use a commission-free real estate service. My bungalow was situated in a quiet residential neighbourhood with quick access to highways, trains, buses, schools, shopping and all amenities, in an area where houses sold rapidly. The property was in an attractive price range and interest rates were very low, making it an ideal home for first-time buyers. I had worn many hats and acquired many skills in this life, raised two wonderful daughters, built a successful consulting practice, published five books—what could be so difficult about selling a house? Plus, several of my clients had urged me to sell the house on my own. Piece of cake, they had said, all of them women with no prior experience in the business. I could do this, I concluded with confidence and eagerness to try my hand at a new skill.

"We really need to talk," the agent said ominously, pointing out that there could be any number of serious problems if I were to sell the house on my own. Not interested in going into full-fledged fear mode, I did not enquire as to the problems that lay in waiting, and instead let the conversation end. Although I did experience faint flutters of fear as I recalled that conversation, each time I reminded myself that it was not a line of thinking that was in keeping with my current goal. Peace was a condition of the Kingdom; this line of thinking would lead to stress, worry, anxiety and fear—that is, loss of peace.

As might be expected, the ego tried its best to paint an enticing picture of drama, fear and worry, but I had learned that I am not the ego and that I am in charge of where I want to place my attention. Grateful for the opportunity to practise making a better choice, I decided to choose peace. The matter would rest in my Father's Hands. Hints of doubt came to mind several times during the day, but each time I said "no." It's in my Father's Hands. With my choice clear and firm, what might ordinarily have turned into a drawn-out sleep-depriving affair simply dissipated as I returned to whatever business was at hand, confident that the Father's Will would be done.

A couple of days later, a second opportunity for fanning the flames of fear arose when I crossed paths with an old acquaintance. I was shopping for a stackable washer and dryer for the condo, my old set having already been promised to the son of a friend who was moving out on his own. During a pleasant exchange of updates, he mentioned that it was a good thing that I was selling my home before the fall elections because, should the wrong party be elected, the market would surely suffer a major downturn. I had not gone into details about my plans for selling the house, avoiding the fact that it was not yet for sale. In fact, I had been aiming for a for-sale date that was close to the election, which could very well have been cause for concern. No, I decided once again, it was in the Father's Hands. *No*, I responded to repeated invitations to worry about the possible consequences of the upcoming elections. I refused to go down that road and instead, I chose peace. That felt much better.

As we know, when friends and family members offer unsolicited counsel, usually it is well intentioned. Nonetheless, if it causes fear, it may indicate that it is coming from their own place of fear. In such cases, one can ask for a positive perspective on the matter at hand but, if such is not forthcoming, then it is entirely appropriate to withdraw from the conversation. Protecting one's own peace of mind always takes priority over giving way to fear. To refuse to engage in fear also teaches the other person that there is a different way of addressing the situation. What comes from fear can never be helpful because it generates a condition of defensiveness, a condition in which faith cannot be fully expressed. In a state of faithlessness, the truth cannot be experienced.

The Alternative to Fear

That summer, I was invited to give a talk on *A Course in Miracles* to a study group in the Eastern Townships. Since most of my misgivings about the teachings of the Course had been ironed out, I felt ready for this task. Having taught and lectured for over 25 years, giving a talk on spirituality and *A Course in Miracles* did not fall in the realm of fear-inducing activities. Quite the contrary; it was a fun and exciting opportunity to share one of my favourite topics. If the ego was going to successfully stir up some fear, it would have to find something else to feed its flames. Resourceful as always, it found the one thing that might serve its purpose. It was actually something that had been building for a number of years—a discomfort that I was beginning to realize had developed into a very real fear.

I had learned to drive in the early 70s with my dad's '68 Oldsmobile 442-Cutlass Supreme. That car was a beast, and as any car enthusiast might imagine, it was awesome to drive. In 1978, I was thrilled to take over ownership of the Cutlass when my dad bought a new car. Back then, driving was fun, not overly stressful and relatively safe. Roads were smoothly paved and because there were far fewer vehicles on the road, drivers generally maintained a comfortable distance between cars.

Over the years, the number of cars increased along with the population but, because Montreal is on an island, major arteries had very little room for expansion. Besides increased congestion and the emergence of massive rush hour traffic jams, the roadways became plagued by potholes and crumbling infrastructures, which meant that during the summer, necessary repairs turned the city into a giant construction zone. Adding to that the fact that many young drivers seemed to have learned to drive while playing video games, driving in the city became less fun, at least for this driver.

Having spent fifteen years working from home in a quiet West Island suburb, with most amenities within walking distance to my home and generally absolved of having to deal with rush hour traffic, I never had the opportunity to update my driving skills to meet the growing challenges of city driving. Although this was not an issue while I travelled in my familiar neighbourhoods, on those rare occasions when I did need to drive into the city, or even just through the city, I experienced anxiety. When I accepted the invitation to speak in the Townships, it became clear that I would have to deal with this limitation since there was no getting around driving through the city if I was to reach my destination. The more I thought about this trip, the more I realized that a very real fear had taken root, and it wasn't about to be easily shaken off.

Once again, I went on an Internet search—a great place for fuelling fear, by the way—and checked out travel and road construction indicators on the Montreal transport website. As I suspected, there were major road repairs scattered throughout the city, in particular on the stretch of highway I would have to pass through to access the bridge. I immediately began to imagine myself shifting and clutching through bottlenecks on the expressway, perhaps even being so sandwiched-in between cars that I would miss an exit and get stuck in a downtown gridlock. As an expression of my need for self-protection, I found a suitable solution: why not take the bus! I ran this idea by the organizer, and she arranged to have someone pick me up at the nearest drop-off point in the Townships. This was a simple enough solution except that it brought up a whole other set of issues. What if I missed one of my connections? Taking the bus required that I also take the train and the metro. Scheduling trains, metros and buses could be tricky. One thing was certain; this route would take four times as long as driving. I was trapped, toggling between two options, overcome by indecision that was clearly motivated by fear. In need of help, I asked for guidance.

"Because you do not perceive yourself as mind does not mean that this is not the truth of what you are. Because you perceive yourself as body does not mean that this is the truth of what you are. In order to perceive yourself in any way different from how you perceive yourself now, you must be curious. First, you must accept that perhaps your perception is not the truth, and then you must be curious to know what the truth about you is, what your true state as spirit is. The simplest and most effective way is to constantly question. What is the truth here? What is beyond what my limited perception serves up for me? Where is spirit? What does the Kingdom of Heaven really look like here, in its fullness, in its wholeness? Since the truth and wholeness and the Kingdom of Heaven have never been altered in any way, they must be here. The only issue at hand is that you still choose not to experience all of it. You still choose, out of habit, out of beliefs—accepted beliefs—to have a limited experience of what you are and what is here."

Clearly, my fear of driving was an indication of my still firm belief in myself as a body. The self seems vulnerable as long as it appears to exist as a body in a world of form. But I was becoming increasingly curious to see beyond the limitations of form; I wanted an experience of my Self as spirit, not just as body. It was understandable that the part of me that still clung to this limited identification as a body would feel threatened. My recognition of my Self as spirit would mean the end of my experience of a separated self, as a body. This was the true meaning of the fear. It was not that I was vulnerable; it was the limited perception of my self as a body that was becoming increasingly fragile while I sought an experience of my true Self. This meant that no matter which option I chose, the ego would find something to achieve its goal of obliterating my comfortable state of peace. In the end, after having checked in with guidance, I decided that the best option would be to drive. Taking the bus was not an efficient use of my time, and I advised the organizer of my change of plan.

As the date for my lecture approached, I found myself reconsidering my decision. Maybe you should take the bus, the ego hinted, nudging me once more into paralyzing indecision. There was only one way to deal with this invitation, and that was to ignore it, to go about my business and trust that I would be safe. That was the only thought worth considering. Flip the switch in my mind, and ask for clarity. To give in to the fear would be to continue to nurture the belief that I am just a body, therefore vulnerable. Not wanting another full-blown ego drama, I asked my friend for more help.

"When you are gripped by fear, in those situations when only fear seems to come to mind, those are the times when, though not easy, it is most effective and powerful to choose to look for what the Father is Being. Images of fear are your personal definitions and expectations being projected into the Kingdom of Heaven. When you remove these fearful images and pictures, which only come from your imagination, you can witness what God is Being. It is a threshold moment where you can experience a glimpse of the truth as opposed to remaining mired in the illusion defined by your projected fear. When you entertain thoughts of fear, what you are doing in effect is interposing a screen between yourself and your awareness of the truth."

I could see that all the thoughts, evaluations and estimations that came from my own thinking interfered with my experience of the truth. If what God is Being is something new at every moment, there is no way that I can guess, project or estimate what God will be Being in the moment. To do so is to put up a barrier and prevent the knowing of what God is Being now. My friend had more to say on the subject.

"How long do you want to postpone having a full experience of what God is Being? Each time you interject with your own interpretations, your own perceptions, your preconceived notions, each time you do this, you delay the full experience of the Kingdom of Heaven. In a world of dreams and illusions, there is a never-ending supply of thoughts, fears, interpretations and definitions that are separate from what God is Being now. Why would you want to wait until you run out of definitions? You will simply continue to make them up as long as you wish to sustain your condition of ignorance and sleep in a dream. Waking up is not a matter of time. Waking up is a decision that you make now in the same way that sleeping in ignorance is a decision that you make now. Everything is in place for you to make a decision to awaken and see the more that is there, just as there are many imagined definitions to keep your attention in the dream."

Despite knowing better, once again, I was tempted to revise my travel arrangements, the argument being that it would be easier to take a bus and that I didn't have to be a hero. Again, I did the only thing there was to do—I dropped the issue. I had made a decision and now it was a matter of trusting that everything in the universe would conspire to make it a safe journey. It was an exercise in trust. I had gone too far with my decision to turn back now. If this was going to be my threshold, then so be it. I was going to walk through it. With my mighty companions by my side, I no longer wanted to acquiesce to fear. I wanted to lean into the strength of the Father. I would have to work hard at pushing away the fears and preconceptions, but I was equal to the task and I was not alone.

A few days before my speaking engagement, while out running errands, I decided to try to see what more there was besides my normal perceptions, what was beyond my conditioned way of looking. I set aside all thoughts of the past, of the errands that had been important enough to get me out of the house and I focused my attention on the moment. Curious, I wanted to know if I could see more than the road, the cars and their drivers. I began to see the flow of cars as though it was a giant ballet, with all of God's Creations flowing to and fro, with order and purpose. Occasionally there might be mishaps, little bumps here and there, just enough to maintain the illusion of danger to our limited perception of ourselves as bodies driving physical cars. Any stress I may have felt while navigating through midday traffic began to leave when I realized that the car was spirit, the road was spirit, that, in fact, everything was spirit. This giant ballet, a harmonious flow of vehicles driven by sons and daughters of God was really spirit and all was flowing in the Kingdom of Heaven. It could only be a safe place.

On the day of my excursion to the Townships, once I had merged onto the highway, I shifted my attention to incorporate All that is there. I tuned into what God was Being, and I saw Life—my brothers and sisters driving their vehicles and flowing in harmony. But more than that, I was aware that each of them was accompanied by the guidance they needed so that their movement could be smooth and harmonious too. Instead of focusing on potential danger and stirring the pot of fear and anxiety, I focused on harmony. It was tentative at first, but then I saw that when I needed to change lanes there was an opening, where I needed to enter or exit the highway, the way was clear.

This isn't to say that I didn't encounter delays on the road that day. In fact, the trip down there took almost twice as long as it should have. The city was effectively a giant construction zone that summer. The trip home was quicker, but there were construction delays on the northbound lanes just as well. Though the entire trip there and back went relatively smoothly, shifting gears through what seemed like hundreds of stops and starts had required my total attention. When I was within a few kilometres of my home, I breathed a deep sigh of relief. It was time to debrief.

What had been the purpose of this exercise? What had I learned? Why had I put myself through this intense process? Had it really been necessary? I examined all of this with Jesus at my side and concluded that it really had not mattered which option I had chosen. If I had made an inappropriate choice, then I would have been guided to make a better choice. What mattered was that I had made a commitment to see it through while managing to ignore the ego's attempts to stir up fear. That was the important point of that particular event, and I was pleased.

As I neared my house, I admitted without reservation that I really did not enjoy driving through the city, and, frankly, there was nothing wrong with that. The more I acknowledged the truth about how I felt, the more I felt at peace. Taking on unnecessary stressful situations was not a requirement for increasing awareness of what God is Being. I knew that the ego could turn around and use this conclusion to make me feel guilty or inadequate. Believe me, it tried. You're a grown-up; you should be able to drive anywhere you want. Don't be such a baby. But, you know what? I didn't want to listen to the ego any more. I would listen to the voice that allowed me to feel at ease and at peace. I did not have to walk tightropes to prove that I was safe and invulnerable. I did not have to push myself to the limit and force myself to overcome fears or anxieties. I could choose simpler, more enjoyable options. But I also knew that if I had to face what seemed to be a difficult situation, I could trust that the Father would be there with me, and all would be well.

This attitude of choosing ease over challenge flew in the face of all of my childhood learning. I had spent a lifetime pushing myself to overcome challenges and obstacles of all sorts. I had committed myself to huge tasks all of my life, and now I was learning that none of it was necessary. Now I realized that there was only one commitment worth making: I wanted to see the more of what God was Being everywhere and in everyone. Since God is Being no matter what is going on, since what God is Being is eternal, whole and safe, I did not have to make any superhuman or heroic efforts.

I just needed to allow what God is Being to simply Be, wherever I was, whatever I was doing.

Following my trek to the Townships, I began to consider selling the car. My condo came with a garage, which I could rent, and with the money saved from insurance and maintenance, I could rent a car, as needed. This idea grew more and more appealing, especially as winter approached. I even signed up online to be notified should a community car service open up in my neighbourhood. Yes, I could sell the car and simplify my life considerably. That was a good plan.

I understood that the goal of awakening is not to achieve or accomplish anything specific in the world. Nonetheless, I had noticed that when I joined with the Father, when I was at peace, things were different. I wanted to understand why it was that parking spots appeared, drivers stopped and allowed pedestrians to cross the street, traffic lights turned green and lane changes were easier when one was in this frame of mind.

"When you have chosen to look for what God is Being while out walking or driving, you are giving your brothers and sisters the opportunity to experience the good that is in them. You are sending an invitation for them to respond in kind. If you go out for a walk with the mindset that you are guilty and not deserving of love, you will go out and project thoughts of guilt, attack or defensiveness in order to find confirmation of your belief. Naturally, those you encounter will respond in kind.

"This is how the world changes; as you decide to shift your attention to Reality, and you begin to experience what is Divine in you, you also invite the experience of what is Divine in your brothers. This leaves the way open, sets the stage and establishes a tone with which your brothers and sisters can respond. It is an invitation to respond in a different way, in a new way, from your place of Divinity. These are not experiences that you consciously seek out. They are the natural consequence of what God is Being in this new moment, when you have decided to allow God to be what He intends for you to be in the moment.

"For these experiences to occur, you must set aside your definitions and your expectations as to what you wish to see occur. Your focus should be on setting aside your meanings and allowing the Divine meaning to express itself, to come, invited by you. This is why you do not change the world by taking action in the world; you change the world by shifting your allegiance to that which is Divine, instead of to what is unreal."

Watching the cars passing by one Sunday, it occurred to me that each person is moving toward their next point of potential awakening, the next event that might challenge their current false limiting beliefs about themselves and about life. At each moment, we are all facing the point that might rattle us just enough to cause us to question, is that all there is? Might there be something else to be experienced? Each person is moving in harmony with his or her own awakening, accompanied by the guidance needed to accomplish this awakening. Awakening is guaranteed because it is our natural condition, and so there can only be one movement, the movement toward awakening.

God goes with me wherever I go. (ACIM.W.41)

Chapter 10

The Right Use of Mind

My mind is part of God's. I am very holy. (ACIM.W.35)

I Have a Mind!

I have a mind; it's that noisy place where all that thinking is going on. While I'm no genius, I do have the ability to think logically and the practical sense to make good use of all the wonderful thoughts generated by this active and, at times, creative mind. At least this is what I used to think. The strong, independent-thinking mind I once valued so highly dropped a couple of notches on my crumbling ladder of significant attributes as a new understanding of mind began to dawn on me. Maybe I still had a mind—we are never mindless—however, having opened up to the possibility that there might be more to it than previously thought, a wholly new way of experiencing reality began to emerge. This new way of seeing was so radically different from what I was familiar with that I had to release everything I once thought to be true, leaving me at times with my head spinning, not knowing anything about anything.

It's not so much the mind itself that was found lacking but rather the manner in which it was being used. In light of my growing new perspective, it became evident that the old way of looking and seeing severely limited my experience of the truth. For a while, it seemed as though I had two minds—a right mind and a wrong mind—with the two never in agreement. However, having two minds is impossible because all minds are expressions of the One Mind of God and must therefore be like their Source—one and whole. It could only be that either I was choosing to use my mind correctly, or I was choosing to use it incorrectly. The choice came from within me, and it was at the point of making a choice that correction could and needed to be made. The big clue as to which choice I had made would always be reflected in the nature of the thoughts that emerged from my mind.

In truth, there is only one right use of mind and only one obstacle to its right use, making the solution quite simple—at least in theory. The question remains always, what do I really want? Since I had been feeling a growing desire for a greater experience of the truth, I would have to take a closer look at what I was actually doing with my mind and clear out the debris of wrong-minded habits. The benefits of seeing the world through the highly personalized, limited lens of the wrong mind or, in the language of *A Course in Miracles*, looking with the ego, were becoming increasingly lost on me. I wanted an experience of the more that is here. To have an experience of Reality would require a radical change in the manner in which I used my beloved mind, a mission that seemed at first daunting and definitely humbling but, in the end, very liberating. I have a mind, yes, but there is another way to use it. It is always a simple matter of choice. What do I really want? That is the important question, because we have no more or no less than what we want.

Thinking Is the Problem

When we are told to use our minds, we generally understand this to mean that we should *think*. Thinking is a highly regarded skill. At home, in school and at church, we were taught to be reasonable, to think things through and be rational. We went to school and studied as best we could to learn from teachers who had learned from teachers of their own. Think for yourself, we were told. Think again! Think it over. Think long and hard. Think big! Think twice about it. As adults, when needed, we hire those who know better than we do. We hold our expert thinkers in very high regard. We defer to our economists, doctors, scientists, researchers—those great minds who know how things work because their findings have been validated in laboratory experiments that can be replicated—and we adopt their ideas. We like to know things; it makes us look good; it makes us feel intelligent. The more stuff we know, the more intelligent we are, the better we look.

Yet, while we are encouraged to pursue all of this wonderful mental activity, our thinking must remain within acceptable parameters or else we run the risk of being corrected by those who know better or, worse, labelled as troublemakers, crazy or even insane. Even when we are invited to "think outside the box," we are limited by a box that has been designated as a valid boundary. Though the designation is usually made by those who have a vested interest in maintaining its existence, it remains in place as long as no one questions it. The fact remains that we are encouraged to think outside the box only if we do not cause the entire box to crumble. If the currently established box were to be proven weak or seriously flawed, then everyone's thinking and understanding would be brought into question. Who wants that! So it is that our boundaries are pushed back bit by bit, only as quickly—and as slowly—as humanity is ready to accept.

Despite our most earnest attempts at correct thinking, we overlook the fact that we—including our experts—are bound by the limited perception and understanding of the moment. Didn't our scientists once teach that the earth was flat and that the sun revolved around the earth? Then again, haven't our physicists postulated that matter is not solid, but is rather a dance of sorts between packets of energy? Yet, who is willing to question the physical nature of the body they haul out of bed or the car they drive to work every morning? Who stops to consider that they might be expressions of energy? With these deeply entrenched beliefs, how are we ever to reach an understanding of ourselves as spirit, let alone pure thought?

And then along comes *A Course in Miracles*, a teaching that is designed to break down our thinking habits; in fact, it causes the box to entirely disintegrate, leaving us to wonder if we ever really knew anything at all! When I first worked my way through the early workbook lessons of the Course, I might as well have been reading the sentences backwards because their meaning was completely lost on me. All I wanted was to get through those first fifty-or-so lessons so I could move on to the more interesting later ones. It wasn't until much later that I came to appreciate that these early lessons were among the most important ones and that some of the later lessons depended on them.

> Nothing I see means anything. I have given everything I see all the meaning it has for me. I do not understand anything I see. I see nothing as it is now. My thoughts do not mean anything. (ACIM.W.1, 2, 3, 9, 10)

Nothing I see means anything—what do you mean, nothing I see means anything? My thoughts do not mean anything—really? To add insult to injury, Raj tells us that *thinking is the evidence of ego!* These statements were an assault on what I thought was a worthwhile activity—*thinking.* Talk about being taken down a couple of notches!

Yet, it is only by accepting to question the validity of current thinking that we can begin to consider that there might be another way of looking and seeing, an invitation that is at the heart of a teaching like the Course. Fortunately, Jesus had a plan when he gave us the big blue book. Not only does it address the undoing of our erroneous thinking habits, it also shows us a better way to use our minds. It teaches the importance of the quiet mind. It is only in the silence within, at the inner altar where the mind is quiet, that the truth can be experienced.

Thinking is a problem because it gets in the way of listening. It is an indicator of the active, wilful use of mind that prevents the full experience of Being. Another problem with active thinking is that it severely limits the mind. The mind is capable of so much more than logical thinking, interpretation, reasoning and making judgments. Thinking uses known information, memories and familiar parameters. It employs a process of interpreting and determining what is going on in the moment based on this very limited information. Thinking that distracts us from the quiet within keeps us from the doorway to the Kingdom of Heaven and therefore serves the ego.

Listening Is the Answer

Very few of us are taught to turn our attention inward, to listen to the inner voice and pay attention to the inspiration that might be helpful for our unfolding. Even less importance is given to the feelings of rightness that lie in waiting for that moment when we might embrace that inner wisdom. With the emphasis on mental activity, we rarely stop to wonder what the quiet silence might have to offer, if anything worthwhile at all. Wanting very much to fit in, sometimes the easiest path is to go along with the accepted thinking of the day. Turning our attention inward seems like hard work at best but, at worst, a potentially terrifying experience. What would happen if we were to turn our attention inward and find nothing? Keeping our attention focused on what seems to be going on in the tangible, material world around us, regardless of what quantum physicists may have to say about it, seems like the safe and appropriate thing to do.

Essential to the greater experience of reality that I earnestly sought was a quiet, listening mind. A quiet mind can only be achieved in the absence of thinking. The absence of thinking can only be achieved by choice, usually as a result of persistent practice. This practice of quiet listening posed a new set of problems. Listening required the setting aside of thinking. In order to set aside thinking, I needed to take a moment to pause and consciously make the decision to set aside thinking. That extra step threw me off my game. Most of my actions were guided by a conscious thinking process. Without this consciously directed thinking, what would happen to all those important things that required my attention? To set aside thinking was also to take a very big risk. It meant giving up control and relinquishing self-derived judgments and conclusions. Above all, setting aside thinking required that I trust that what I needed to know would come to me, without any conscious direction or wilfulness on my part.

Having grown adept at thinking for myself, it would take a fair amount of practice before the new habit of being quiet and listening—that is, not thinking—could be developed and practised at all times. Thinking was one of the activities that I found most valuable. There was always something brewing in the back of my mind concerning one important matter or other. I ran a business, met with clients, wrote books and maintained a house. There was no shortage of situations to be addressed, and all of these activities required thinking, planning and a fair share of problem solving. Admittedly, being able to attend successfully to all of these matters did provide a sense of accomplishment and satisfaction.

Not only was thinking second nature, it also served a couple of very important, though perhaps less obvious, functions. First, it made a case for my existence. I think, therefore, there must be somebody here! It must follow that the more I think, the more significant is this somebody. The next important function of thinking is that it kept the frightening spectre of its opposite at bay—silence. The more noise, the less chance there was of being swallowed up into the dark, silent abyss that held only the promise of judgment, condemnation and inevitable annihilation. Besides, thinking was fun, it kept me busy and it helped pass the time. What was one to do in the absence of thoughts? Quick, what's the next problem requiring my attention!

To take the time to be quiet and listen has another important function: it reflects a willingness to join. To listen is to be open to something or someone other than oneself. Each thought, each action that arises from separate, independent thinking reinforces the belief in the idea of separation. To pause and consciously join is one of the most powerful statements of the desire to awaken. It says, I am not alone, I wish to be partnered and I will not rely entirely on my own independent will.

The Function of Mind

I was on the verge of putting my house up for sale, trying to settle on a price and growing a bit anxious about the whole business. There was a whole lot of illusion on my plate, and I was thinking that I would have been more comfortable living in a cave in Tibet. There was a whole lot of thinking to be done and it was beginning to mess with my peace of mind. If independent thinking is to be abandoned and replaced by listening, what then is the function of mind? What do I do with my nicely honed thinking apparatus? Is thinking ever okay? More importantly, how does one go about regular life? I had lots of questions, and so I checked in with my friend.

"To dismiss the world, your job or anything that is confronting you or that you are perceiving is to say that there is something that is not worthy of your attention. It is to say that there is a hierarchy of illusions. Instead, practise asking to see the truth instead of dismissing what is perceived. What does this thing truly mean? What is God Being in this thing? To say that it is an illusion is not quite accurate. The illusion comes from your misperception, your limited ability to recognize what a thing truly is. Ask to experience the truth that is beyond your limited or illusory interpretation of what is there, because, in truth, there is something there, in truth there is God Being, there is Life, there is Creation. The only problem is that you have decided to give it your own interpretation, your own meaning, your own definition.

"The reason the Course says that you see only the past is because what you are perceiving is the result of processing data according to what you want to experience. If you simply allow something to come to your awareness, it will tell you what is its significance and purpose. Otherwise, what you are doing is assigning your own meaning to what comes to you through perception. This is *you* interfering with what God is Being, what Creation is Being. This is *you* not allowing Being to occur. It is *you* controlling your experience so that it will conform to your desire or your wish. This validates once again that you have the experience you decided you were going to have. To see the All that is there, one must also be free of the desire to see things in a certain way, usually in a way that reinforces cherished beliefs.

"Give up, abandon the meanings you have given to everything, and allow the truth of what is there to be revealed, to come through, so that you can have a more truthful or meaningful experience of everything that you perceive, everything that is confronting you, everything that you encounter, everything that is within your range of experience. After you have asked to see the meaning of what is there, be silent, be quiet, listen and be attentive. Once you have removed your personal definitions, you can then pay attention.

"The right use of mind is to be pay attention, to be in a state of conscious awareness. In order to be able to pay attention, one must be free of senseless mental chatter. Where you place your attention will determine your experience. If you want a different experience, shift your attention to another direction. Remember, the function of the mind is to pay attention.

"Thoughts are not the problem. Listening does not mean becoming devoid of thoughts, nor stopping or controlling the flow of thoughts. It means that the thoughts that arise will be a consequence of the natural flow of your Being rather than from the small separated self whose sole purpose is to claim and validate its existence.

"There is a tendency to want to help things along, whereas all that is needed is for you to simply pay attention and listen. You will know what needs to be done. Allow the unfolding to occur. You are not being asked to refrain from doing. You are simply being asked to pay attention to what is the appropriate doing. In that way, you will participate in the unfolding. Your experience will be much smoother, less bumpy. You will encounter fewer obstacles. You will feel yourself flowing with your life principle, rather than struggling with life. You will also feel yourself participating and very much accompanied. You will not be alone.

"In this frame of mind or attitude, any thinking that occurs arises from inspiration. It serves to facilitate your flowing. You do not need to think about what to do or think to solve problems. There are no problems to be solved. There is nothing to do other than be aware of the unfolding.

"The experience of awakening means accessing a part of the mind that appeared to be previously inaccessible. This does not refer to a part of the thinking, cognitive mind that you work very hard at training and developing. This is the Mind that is the One Mind from which Creation emanates. It is the only place of true awareness. A limited, separate mind—the independent thinking mind—is simply a substitute and its power and creative ability pale in comparison to that of the Whole Mind. When you reaffirm, or reassert, your relationship and connection with the One Mind, you return to your natural state of wholeness and access true creativity. You are then no longer limited by conventions or past and present learning, convictions and beliefs.

"By engaging curiosity, you can suspend thinking and applying your own meaning to what is being perceived, and in that moment of suspension, you allow what is really there to reveal itself to you."

Decisions, Decisions

Most of us fall prey to a little indecision now and then; for some, it may even be one of those secret guilty pleasures. Having something to fuss, worry and think about keeps us focused on something other than what truly matters, that dangerous quiet centre within. What I was learning is that when I am focused on the quiet centre, there is no need for senseless thinking. Indecision is like a perpetual motion machine, continuing indefinitely on its own steam until, from sheer exhaustion, we decide that we've had enough and we find something else to fuss over. It is the perfect device for keeping us from quiet listening, a well-used device in my ego's armoury.

Being an avid planner, it wasn't long before I had directed all of my pertinent know-how and resources to the move to the condo. An architectural drafting course I had taken decades earlier combined with extensive computer skills allowed me to play around with design and decorating layouts for my new home. Moving into a small living space required some careful planning, and planning was one of my favourite mental sports. The trick would be to learn to distinguish between senseless distracting planning and inspired purposeful planning. The former serves to keep attention focused outward; the latter simply flows from my Being within. Given the scope of this move, on a number of occasions I fell prey to mindless indecision, worry and confusion. Following is a collection of helpful tips I received on how to deal with this chronic condition.

"When faced with a situation in which you are feeling indecisive, you are trying to figure things out on your own—without guidance.

In order to hear guidance, your mind has to be quiet. You must be at peace and you must be ready to relinquish your desire to be wilful. You must abandon your wilfulness and be in a state of acceptance and surrender. Only then can guidance come. If you are tossing up two or three options, you are in your own separated individual mind and working from individual will. That is, the problem is not the choice between three options; the problem is that you are using individual will. By abandoning individual will, you allow guidance that is more knowledgeable than your individual will to enter. While individual will serves the individual, guidance serves all.

"When feeling indecisive, flip-flopping between two or more options, a good approach is to simply let go of the question or the issue for the time being. Do nothing. If a decision needs to be made, the issue will decide itself for you; your solution will come. If you make a decision from a place of indecisiveness, tossing options back and forth, you are likely to make a decision that does not best suit your current need. Lay it aside and trust that the decision will be made clear for you. If action is required, you will know precisely what to do. You will know that this is the right thing to do because it will come to you from a place of peace and quiet and perhaps some joy and curiosity about what will be coming next.

"Indecision is nothing more than a clever form of ego distraction. There is always only one correct choice to make and that is to allow what God is Being: Father, let Thy Will be done. In releasing the activity of indecisiveness, the correct course of action will be revealed in a form that is appropriate and in a time frame that is appropriate.

"The distress or the confusion is never about what appears to be going on. The only thing that can be distressed is the ego, and what frightens the ego the most is change. The ego likes a situation it can control. It likes to make the changes it decides it is going to make. If you embark on a journey of awakening with *A Course in Miracles* or any other teaching, you will be putting the ego in a position of not knowing. When it does not know what is coming up, it does not have control, and anxiety and fear will be expressed.

"When you are aware of your wholeness, when you are aware of your invulnerability, there is never any reason for fear or anxiety; peace prevails in the right mind. Only in the wrong mind can there be anything but peace. Indecision, toggling between options and confusion over choices belong to the same category. From peace comes knowing; from knowing comes right doing. In peace, there are no questions, doubts or uncertainties. Indecision is the result of thinking and analysis, not of coming from a place of inner peace."

When in Doubt, Do Nothing!

When I began the practice of abandoning thinking in favour of listening, one of the first things I learned was that much of my thinking and mental busyness was not even necessary. Not only did thinking interfere with the capacity to hear inspiration and guidance, it also interfered with the capacity to experience Being. Given that old habits die hard, this would require dedicated practice and perseverance. As a first step in learning to deal with my delinquent mind, I adopted a very simple practice. Whenever overcome by indecision or uncertainty, I engaged in doing nothing. Although this was an unusual practice for an avid doer, I soon found it to be surprisingly effective. Doing nothing became one of my favourite ways of putting an end to tiresome mental battles, something that occurred frequently as I was going through the thousands of steps leading up to the big move. If a situation became overly complicated, I'd leave it alone, be quiet, turn my attention elsewhere, put my mind on something simple and trust that a solution would come. I had learned that if I really needed to do something or be somewhere, I would be nudged in that direction. My new motto was: when in doubt, do nothing.

A few months before moving to the condo, I embarked on the very special quest of finding the best shower curtain for my new bathroom. It was a very stressful period, as I was faced with the uncertainty of selling my house on time, the possibility of rising interest rates and whatever other fear-producing concerns the ego could send my way. For some insane reason, it seemed important that I find a curtain with a bamboo-like design in shades of soft browns to balance the dark espresso bathroom vanity. Go figure. The ego does at times lack subtlety. This mindless quest rapidly turned into an obsession as I scoured the Internet and made trips to all the local stores that sold shower curtains. I even brought one home only to discover that in the daylight the colours were quite different from those under the artificial lighting of the store. Even though the design was close to what I had in mind, the greenish hue didn't work, and so back to the store it went. This senseless quest continued for several weeks, before I finally decided to give up. This was a waste of time and definitely not peace inducing. When in doubt, do nothing. And so, finally, I did nothing, at least with regards to ferreting out the perfect shower curtain.

I think someone "Upstairs" took pity on me, because a few days later I woke up with the clear idea that I should return online to one of my favourite shopping spots. When I typed in the keywords "shower curtains," the first one to pop up was a bamboo design in soft browns. I came to see that this mad quest for the perfect shower curtain had been a desperate attempt to cling to some element of control while my life was being deconstructed from top to bottom. If I couldn't control the sale of the house or the move to the condo or my process of awakening, I could at least control which shower curtain I purchased!

> Peace is the bridge that everyone will cross, to leave this world behind. But peace begins within the world perceived as different, and leading from this fresh perception to the gate of Heaven and the way beyond. Peace is the answer to conflicting goals, to senseless journeys, frantic, vain pursuits, and meaningless endeavors. Now the way is easy, sloping gently toward the bridge where freedom lies within the peace of God. (ACIM.W.200)

Chapter 11

Listen to the Feeling

There is one thought in particular that should be remembered throughout the day. It is a thought of pure joy; a thought of peace, a thought of limitless release, limitless because all things are freed within it. (ACIM.M.16)

The Value of Feelings

For as long as I can remember, I cannot recall ever having been taught, let alone encouraged, to value feelings. Expressions of emotion were generally met with disapproval, which is interesting considering that the entire ego system was set up to instill a profound fear of God and all things powerful and authoritative. This early environment was not designed to inspire a healthy curiosity for what might exist outside the box. It followed naturally that it was not appropriate to include feelings as a valid criterion for making important life decisions.

Although the main function of mind is to pay attention, sometimes words are not sufficient to convey the full meaning of what is being experienced. As I released my need for intellectual understanding and began to practise paying attention, I became aware of just how many times the only way to capture the full meaning of an experience is through feelings. For example, the beauty of a work of art such as a painting, a poem or a piece of music is not fully appreciated by intellect alone; one might say that art is experienced with the heart. Unfortunately, I'm the furthest thing from being an artist. While my mother kept the radio tuned to the local classical station, my dad strummed classical and flamenco airs on his Spanish guitar, and my brother played Debussy and Rachmaninoff on the piano, I played my James Brown LP on my record player. Being a rational, intellectual and non-artistic person, it would take me a bit longer to appreciate the importance of paying attention to feelings.

Raj makes a very clear distinction between feelings and emotions. Emotions, he points out, are ego reactions, while feelings are Soul's recognition of itself in what it is experiencing. He describes the Soul as the sensing organ of the mind, giving the mind a whole new function. I was familiar with emotions such as fear, grief and anxiety, just as I was familiar with joy and exhilaration. It just never occurred to me that there was a difference between feelings and emotions, even less that feelings could be helpful in recognizing the truth. I received additional snippets of insight from my friend.

"Feelings are the Soul's means of communicating. They tell you what is going on from inside and may serve to inspire right action. Emotions are ego responses to what is going on; they serve to propel you into reaction.

"You have used your intellect to learn that there is more to your experience than what you have experienced in the past. Now is the time to complete the experience by including the *feeling*. You know that the Kingdom of Heaven is right here, right now. To have a complete experience of this you must allow yourself to feel it. Intellectual understanding is not sufficient. True knowledge includes feeling; allow the feeling."

I became concerned about feelings I sometimes experienced during meditation. I had been practising complete surrender, letting myself fall, as though into the Arms of God. There were moments when I was overcome by shudders of total release, similar to the release that occurs during orgasm. I felt somewhat ashamed and wondered if I was doing something wrong. As might be expected, my friend had a few words to say.

"You have an absurd and entirely baseless belief that pleasure is a bad thing. Many of your religions have built this into their teachings. Naturally, as perceived from the ego's perspective, if there was something more pleasurable than catering to your misperceptions and your false beliefs, even the valued pain of the ego, it would tell you not to pay attention to it. And the only thing better than all the misperceived pleasures of the world is the pleasure of Being entirely what God is Being in you now. It can only be an enjoyable experience and can only feel good. What is of God can only *be* good."

I have to admit that it did take a while before I returned to my meditation practices. In the meantime, more and more feelings of joy did manage to seep through the ego's defences, especially when I let go and allowed myself to be in the Presence of God.

Finding Peace

How can I effectively deal with a challenging situation when I have tried everything—meditation, going for a walk, taking a hot bath— the things that usually work, but I still can't find peace? What if I just can't help but feel upset? This is a common experience that clients shared with me and I passed on to our friend.

"As soon as is conveniently possible, give yourself permission to choose a peace-inducing activity. If peace is your goal, then you should do whatever it takes to eliminate or avoid that which is contrary to peace. Be more committed to establishing peace than you are to experiencing conflict.

"In situations in which you find yourself completely overwhelmed by emotions such as grief, fear, resentment, anger, frustration, guilt, etc., and find it next to impossible to establish a condition of peace, the simplest and most effective solution is to find something enjoyable to do. Find an activity that will take your mind off the drama. Take the dog for a walk, play a video game with your child, go for a drive in the countryside, paint the hallway, go to the gym, wash the windows of your house, shampoo the interior of your car, vacuum the house, mow the lawn, eat cake and ice cream, or go to the movies. Do anything that will take your mind off the situation.

"The important thing is not what you do; it doesn't matter whether you shampoo the car or play a game of tennis with your neighbour. What matters is that you have consciously said "no" to the disruptive thinking. If the thoughts return, go for another round of tennis, wash the exterior of the car or play with the dog. Do this until you recognize that it is *you* who makes the decision as to where your attention will be focused. Do you want to experience anger, resentment, grief or guilt, or do you want to be joyful, peaceful and open to experiencing what the Kingdom of Heaven has in store for you today? How you feel will attest to what you really want to experience.

"Now, you may say that this sounds childish, and distraction is indeed a common practice employed with children who are behaving in a less-than-orderly fashion. You may say that this would amount to little more than avoidance of your responsibilities, and that grown-ups must face situations at hand. Since your question concerns how to deal with thoughts that arise from seeming events in a dream, ask yourself, how sane is it to "deal" with situations in a dream? In a fantasy?"

This sounds like avoidance of responsibility and other people may not think this to be acceptable. Besides, I told my friend, I'd probably have the cleanest car on the block!

"This is not a lack of responsibility. If this is what you think, ask yourself, for what or for whom am I really responsible? If, as *Course in Miracles* students often like to say, "The world out there is just an illusion," then how can you say that to go wash the car instead of further engaging in conflict with a brother is an irresponsible act? If the world is an illusion, then the reason for the conflict must be an illusion. How long do you wish to maintain illusory responsibility for an equally illusory condition of conflict, guilt, grief or suffering?

"If you go away and wash the car, you may be concerned that others will see you as running away from a situation. Remember always that your first responsibility is to your Self. That is the "you" that is real. That is the "you" to which you need to answer—your Self. Since this Self is One with all of Creation, then in being attentive to the requirements of your Self, you will have honoured your responsibility for all your brothers and sisters, since all minds are joined. When you are at peace, you are connected with your Self. This is where you need to be. To shift your focus from guilt or any other distracting thought to peace is your primary responsibility.

"Others may see this as avoidance of responsibility only because this is how you have mutually defined responsibility. In a world defined by brothers and sisters whose understanding is limited by an ego-based foundation, conflict is dealt with in certain customary ways. Within the ego frame of reference, it is not customary to deal with distress by simply deciding to say "no" to it. In fact, going off to wash the car instead of dealing with your perceived problem could be judged as conflict avoidance or denial.

"In your made-up world, you make much of dealing with conflict in healthy and acceptable ways. There is a whole science built around dealing with conflict. There are books that teach you how to handle difficult people, situations and events. What you do not realize is that dealing with and handling conflict makes conflict real. If conflict is part of life in the dream, then it too is illusory. Would you attempt to resolve a situation that occurred in a dream you had last night? Don't deal with it or try to fix it; ignore it and look for what is real instead. Remind yourself that as a son or daughter of God, your birthright is to be joyful, peaceful and conflict-free. Being conflict-free is not only for diamonds!

"There is a very clever, underlying component to this question, courtesy of your ego frame of reference. By stating that you can't get rid of your unwanted thoughts, you are implying that you are a victim of circumstances, of your actions. This too is insane, since you choose the thoughts you desire to have. You are not ever a victim of your thoughts! By declaring that you 'can't find peace,' you are implying that you are a helpless victim of these thoughts that prevent you from experiencing peace. It would be more honest to say that, at least at this moment, you simply don't want peace. The truth is that you can choose to be at peace at any given moment, and that no matter the circumstances, this remains true. If you are not at peace, it is because you have chosen to experience something other than peace, such as fear, guilt, sadness, anger or resentment. Notice that the substitutes for peace are numerous. However, there is only one appropriate substitute for lack of peace, and that is peace. Since you are the chooser of your thoughts and therefore the determiner of your experiences, you are never a victim of your thoughts, nor of your circumstances.

"This is a very practical approach to increasing your experience of peace, an essential ingredient to awakening. Remember that it is never about what you do, whether you wash the car or practise yoga. What matters is that you have consciously, with full awareness, said "no" to the impediments to your experience of peace. Peace is a condition of the Kingdom of Heaven; you cannot awaken without it. This is the truth. To say no to conflict or lack of peace is to deny the denial of truth. This is not a lack of responsibility; it is an act of Self-respect. It is a very responsible act."

The Destabilized Ego

It was beginning to dawn on me that only the ego-identified self can be upset; the peaceful mind can only experience truth, beauty and wholeness. To catch myself when I was upset might not be such a bad thing after all, because it would mean that I was aware of my choice, even on the threshold of a greater awareness.

"The reason why when you are the most upset you are on the threshold of awakening is because there is only one part of you that can be upset, and that is the ego, and when it is upset it is because it feels threatened. It is destabilized; it has lost control. In its destabilized state, you are in the best position to ask to see the more that is there. When it is destabilized, it has less power, less hold over your perceptions, despite your belief to the contrary. When the ego is destabilized, when it has drawn you into the world and is getting your attention very loudly, you can still go to the quiet place within and decide that you will not pay attention to it. This is the best way to weaken its hold on you. When you choose peace instead of paying attention to the destabilizing event, the ego further loses its hold; you are responding less and less to that which is not the truth; you are choosing to respond to truth instead. This is the very practical aspect of the process of awakening."

Dancing with My Father

Do what you love—a bit of advice I sometimes give to clients who are stuck in a rut, a helpful cure-all for whatever ails you. Just do what you love. In September of that big year of endings, in a 9 month, I decided to do something I loved. Being a numerologist, I knew better than to start something new in a 9 month of endings, but I guess I didn't want to go with the knowing that day. It was a 3 day, a social day, a fun day, a joie-de-vivre day and I felt good as I walked to Mary Queen of Peace Church for an evening of dance lessons. A little cha-cha and rumba could only be fun. I deserved a little joy in my life.

This was typically an activity for partners, but the ad had said "Social Dance, with or without partner," so I decided to give it a chance. When I arrived at the sign-up table, I let the woman know that I did not have a dance partner. I had other partners, but it didn't seem appropriate to tell her that I had walked over with Jesus, Mary, God and whoever else was tagging along that night. I was assured that it was not a problem, that there were usually at least a couple of men without partners. If not, I would be partnered with the assistant teacher.

It was a small class, seven couples and me, the odd one in the bunch. The teacher started by demonstrating the basic merengue step. Two more steps and we had a short routine. When it was time to practise with music, he sent the male assistant to dance with me. Before a new step was added, the second assistant teacher approached me.

"You've danced before?" she asked.

"Yes," I replied, "but many years ago." I was quite content to be in a beginner class—no pressure, just fun.

She informed me that there was a gentleman at their other school who was looking for a partner. She would invite him to join us the following week.

We had practised our routine for another ten minutes, when, this time, the main teacher approached me and asked me the same question. I gave him the same answer.

"There's a man sitting on the bench back there who's just here to watch," he explained. "It seems he's danced before. Maybe he will be your partner for this class."

Busy counting steps and trying to remember the new routine, I hadn't noticed anyone else in the room. This would free up the assistant to help other dancers, so I accepted his proposal.

"I'll go ask him," the teacher said, and off he went to fetch me a dance partner.

Before the next dance step was demonstrated, I was introduced to my new partner. There I stood, five foot six, taller with dance shoes, more comfortable in yoga clothes than dance gear, facing my new partner, a five foot five retiree from Ceylon called Derek. I was about to learn that a dancer should not be judged by his shoes any more than a book should be judged by its cover. Not only could Derek dance, he could also lead, which is not an easy skill for a male dancer to master. Each time the teacher changed the music and called a new dance, Derek exclaimed, "I love this music, I love this music." It was fun and amusing, and I had a wonderful time. Though Derek had not danced in twelve years, he clearly had the moves, having been a competitive dancer. To return the favour, I stayed for the advanced class as partner for Derek from Ceylon.

Walking home that night, I felt completely safe, guided and protected. This was Mary's church, I lived in Jesus' parish and this was the Kingdom of Heaven. I was overwhelmed by a feeling of belonging such as I had never felt before. In my meditation that night, I knew that more than anything in the universe, I wanted to experience the Father's perspective. That's all that really mattered now, because I knew in my heart that nothing else was of value. My Father would tend to all my needs.

When I woke up the following morning, I felt great. There was a bit of tightness in my joints, which I stretched out with some sun salutations. Even my arm didn't hurt when I raised it to pull on my sweatshirt, which was interesting, since I had held up my frame for two dance classes the previous night. How else could I have felt? I had been in Mary's church. In the end, I understood that the evening had not been about the dance; it had been about allowing myself to follow a suggestion and then feeling the safety and the love of the guidance from which it came.

I'm not quite sure what triggered the downward spiral I stumbled into over the days that followed, but one thing is certain, compared to all of my previous dark passages, this one had to be the most frightening. Actually, it seemed that each new dark passage was worse than the last. No doubt, my increasing embrace of the possibility of awakening was once again stirring up equally intense resistance from the still ego-identified portion of my mind. On another of my ill-fated Internet searches, I became aware of individuals whose works had been "officially" authenticated. It was nearly impossible to reject the ego's very convincing invitation to consider that perhaps my work with guidance might be all made up by yours truly. *You think you're communicating with Jesus? Really! Now, Mary? Double really!* Though I rejected the invitation to pursue this dim avenue as best I could, somehow the darkness stuck like black on tar, obscuring my newly expanding way of experiencing life. With confidence in my journey taking a sudden nosedive, I forgot to join with guidance as I went about my daily business. Fortunately, even though I forgot to join with my friend, he never forgot about me.

"Limited vision is simply a consequence of deciding to be separate from your Source. The only way to be separate from the Source is to attach your experience of self to the physical or perceptual realm of your Being. The reason you have felt uncomfortable the last couple of days is that you have forgotten to ask, or you have less consistently asked to see, what is the truth here. Limited perception is the result of a habitual practice of looking independently of what the Father is Being. It is simply the result of a habit. The need now is to continue with the practice of asking the Father, "What is the more to be experienced here?" Your awakening will be the result of your persistent willingness to see the more that is there but also your persistent willingness to not accept the limited form of seeing that you are accustomed to. Simply replace the old habit of accepting limited vision as a satisfactory form of seeing with the new habit of being curious to see what is beyond the limited form. Make a new habit of your curiosity.

"Your recent feelings of isolation and aloneness are simply a reflection of your increasing awareness of, or sensitivity to, the fact that you are really not alone. When you forget that you are not alone and return to being as though you were alone, this creates a greater sense of aloneness. It is simply an indication of your heightened awareness. You are more acutely aware now of the darkness, the cold that is experienced when you forget to walk with the Father, when you practise being autonomous. Remember always that your Being is not an independent act. Your Being comes always from the Father. You simply allowed doubt to temporarily slip in, and in your moment of doubt you reverted to your customary way of being, which is independent from the Father, your Source.

"Being independent, being separate, no longer feels good now that you have experienced moments of joining. And it will continue to feel increasingly uncomfortable. The only solution now is to persist in practising joining in all circumstances. Bring this practice out of your meditations, out of your quiet times, into the world, in all circumstances, whether familiar or unfamiliar."

The following week, after a hectic workday, I attended a second dance class. Again, I was partnered with an eager Derek. At the end of the advanced class, he suggested that we should practise three or four times a week, listing off some of his favourite clubs around town. I realized that signing up for dance class with my life in such turmoil probably had not been the most practical thing to do at this time. Given my busy schedule, there was very little time for practice. Besides, Derek deserved someone who could devote as much time as he was prepared to devote to practice. Nonetheless, we did have an enjoyable evening.

On the way home, I took my usual shortcut through the parking lot along the train station platform. One of the streetlights was out and it was very dark. There were other functional lights ahead and behind, but somehow I felt swallowed up by the darkness. As I continued on my way home, the sense of darkness increased, following me into the house, staying with me during my evening meditation and as I settled for bed. I felt completely alone—devoured by a desolation I had not felt for over forty years. I was alone in my house, alone in my life, alone on my journey. I had fallen into a dark pit of despair, and as I looked ahead to life in a condo, the feeling of isolation intensified. I felt completely disconnected from the Presence of God and it was the worst feeling in the world. I meditated for an hour before going to sleep, and still I couldn't shake it.

It was clear that over the previous few days, busy with the stuff of everyday life, once again, I had forgotten to join with my helpers, and, above all, I had forgotten to join with the Father. *You don't love yourself enough*, I heard my friend say as I lay my head on my pillow. I called on Mary and Jesus and I prayed to the Father that I never ever again feel that kind of aloneness. Never, ever again, I declared with the totality of my Being.

Upon waking up the following morning, I was delighted to find that the darkness in my heart and Soul had dissipated. "From now on, you dance with *Me*," I heard very clearly. There was no doubt in my heart that the Father was with me, and He would never abandon me. As I began the deep breathing and slow warm-ups of my yoga routine, I was filled with great peace and joy.

In time, with practice, you will never cease to think of Him, and hear His loving Voice guiding your footsteps into quiet ways, where you will walk in true defenselessness. For you will know that Heaven goes with you. (ACIM.W.153)

Chapter 12

Mind, Body, Spirit

Spirit am I, a holy Son [Daughter] of God, free of all limits, safe and healed and whole, free to forgive, and free to save the world. (ACIM.W.97)

Sometimes, when I need to reconnect with my centre, I remind myself that I am a thought in the Mind of God. But, while in the middle of selling the house, replacing furniture, preparing to move to a dwelling that wasn't even built, over and above the daily business of ordinary life, it was difficult to see myself as "a thought." I might have been able to work with the *idea* that I am spirit and that I am not *really* a body, but I was stuck with the undeniable experience of *having* a body and being trapped in a world filled with forms and bodies of all kinds. Then there was the inescapable fact of having to deal with an ageing body and its varied aches and pains. It was difficult to imagine how it was possible to live in a body *and* be spirit or thought or whatever it is that I am. Why was it so difficult to relinquish this identification with form? If the body is an illusion, why does it feel so real? What happens to the body when you awaken? Besides my cherished household possessions, I was also faced with the challenge of releasing a number of deeply rooted and long-held beliefs, the most obdurate being that I have a body.

Over a period of several months, once again, I shared these and similar questions with Jesus. Following are some of the answers I received, many of which came while I was out on my daily walks, some during meditation and others upon waking up in the morning. Fortunately, my friend—our friend—is blessed with the gifts of infinite patience, unlimited love and kindness. By simply asking for help, we have the opportunity to experience these wonderful gifts first-hand.

"Ever since the moment you decided to join your brothers and sisters in this make-believe dream world, you forgot what you really are—*spirit*. You felt this was necessary in order to make your participation in the dream complete. And although it has been helpful to forget what you truly are, in the sense that it has facilitated your complete understanding of what it is like to live in ignorance, it does not follow that you must live in ignorance for the rest of your life. It is possible to live in the world *and* know the truth.

"Ignorance is not a requirement for completing your life in the world in a body. You can have the full knowledge of what you are— spirit. What you are lacking is faith. What you are clinging to is self-loathing, which is a natural experience when one chooses total ignorance. Continue to be curious about the more that is there. Extend that to include curiosity about your true Self. What is beyond your limited self? What is your Self truly like? Be curious to know that. It is possible for you to remember the truth while still appearing to manifest a body. Manifesting a physical form to complete your experience with your brothers and sisters does not require that you be ignorant of your Self as spirit. Expect to know yourself as spirit because it is your natural condition. Continue to look for what God is Being in you, because God has never ceased *Being* in you. That is the only worthwhile pursuit. Everything else will fall into place if you make this your sole pursuit.

"You have developed the excellent habit of looking for what God is Being outside of you, for what God is Being in your brothers and your sisters, for what God is Being on the street as you walk. But, once again, you continue to ignore what God is Being in *you*. Ask yourself, what is God Being in *me*? God is Being *love* in you. God is Being *wholeness* in you. God is Being what is *good* in you. The ignorance that says otherwise can be easily discarded. Just push it aside; change the dial on the radio. Look for another song, the song of what God is Being in you. Father, what is the truth Being in me? What you have learned can now be applied to yourself."

It is true that it was becoming increasingly easy for me to see "the good"—that which is whole—in others. This was particularly the case in consultation work, where a greater awareness of the truth of what God was Being in my brothers and sisters was beginning to emerge. Sometimes, after a client left my office, I would simply remain in awe of the beauty and the wonder of what we had shared together. Despite these moments of revelation, I still didn't feel much like I was spirit, let alone whole and perfect. It is true that I saw wholeness emerging in others but not in myself.

"The pain and tension you feel in your body is an alarm. It's a sounding bell, a warning. There is no need to pay attention to the alarm. When the doorbell rings, do you analyze the sound of the ring of the doorbell? No. You go to the door, you open the door and you greet whoever is there or you sign for a package or you donate some money to a local charity, but you don't stand there and analyze the ring of the doorbell. It is the same with your body now. You don't analyze the pain and the tension in your body; you pay attention to the sound of the bell and you go to the door. What is the door? The door is your mind.

"The alarm is saying stop doing something that is not right. What is it that you are doing that is not right? You are continuing to cling to the limited perception of yourself as a form. You are clinging to that belief and you are projecting your own self-hatred onto it. You are beating it up; you are making it real. You are trying to prove that you are a guilty daughter of God, that you have separated and that you are not deserving of wholeness and peace. You cling to the belief that you are not deserving of experiencing the All of what you are as God created you. You are clinging to this false, limited view of yourself.

"The alarm is saying there is more to you than this body. But, at the same time, do not hate the body or demean it; it is part of who you are. It is the visible, tangible aspect of God expressing Himself through you. You must love it too. The alarm says, turn now and look for the more that is you. Embrace all of what you are as God's Expression. Love all of what you are as God's Expression. When you love all of what you are, the body can only reflect wholeness. The body then will not feel limiting, creaking, ageing, painful and stiff. It will simply serve its purpose—which is to allow you to function in a world in which your brothers and sisters continue to cling to the limited perception of who they are also. Give the body a wholly new purpose. Allow it to serve God.

"As long as your body is used as an object onto which your ego can project self-hatred, it serves a very important function, and will remain in its seemingly physical condition. As you love yourself, as you remove all self-hatred, it will no longer serve the ego's purpose and so your identification of yourself as body or form will be released.

"To believe that you are a body is the result of a habit of thinking that you are a body. In order to release yourself from this habit, simply create a new habit of looking for the truth of what you are—spirit, whole, the tangible, visible expression of what God is Being in you. Before you can fully experience this, you need to practise turning toward the mind, or the altar within.

"Your body, as a physical object, is a perceptual event, something that occurs in your mind; it is the physical and tangible representation of your Self. As a separated Christ, you choose to limit your experience of yourself to this perceptual event to the exclusion of the full light and spirit that you truly are. To glorify God is to seek to experience the fullness of your Being, which is nothing less than an expression of God's Love. You are more than this body.

"The physical form appears to exist as long as you limit your experience to your perceptions. At this time, this is the only means you have of connecting with what is really occurring, which is God Being love, which is the true meaning of Creation. You will continue to have perceptual experiences as long as it serves purpose, so that you can join with your brothers in a way that is effective.

"Your seeming experience as a body is nothing more than a thought. It is a thought that says, let me be separate from my Father, let me be separate and unique from my brothers. This limited experience of yourself as a body is not natural and a lot of effort is required to maintain it. As real as it appears, it has never been real and it will never be real. You have maintained this thought to the exclusion of your memory of the truth.

"Your memory of the truth has long been obscured by your habit of thinking of yourself as separate from the Father, a separate entity encased in physical form. Yet, nothing has changed. Your true Self as spirit remains undamaged, always whole and loved. To experience your true Self, all that is needed is the willingness to have that experience. Trust that it will come to you—you *will* have it. Trust the process of letting go of your false, limited perception of yourself.

"By being willing to relinquish your limited perception of yourself, you will begin to remember more and more your true Self, the Self that is awake and has never been otherwise. When you spend time worrying about the body, and that includes everything that relates to its survival and comfort—the house, food, money—you are reinforcing your belief in this made-up version of yourself. Your thoughts are on sustaining the separate self, the illusion of separation. Your thoughts are not on uncovering the truth of who you are. Whenever this occurs—and remember that this is always just a habit of thinking—be vigilant for these thoughts, catch yourself and, as with everything else that comes from the ego framework, simply flip the switch and ask, Father, what is the truth? Spirit does not need to worry about its survival. It does not have to be defensive or fearful. When you are fearful for the survival of the body, you are fearful for something that is not real. There is no need, ever, to be fearful. Flip the switch.

"The cause of all of this questioning about the body, the seeming world of form and all of its needs is a wish to have an experience of independence, of separation from perfect Oneness. That is all that sustains this idea of body and form. It is just a thought, a wish. Look at the wish without fear. Eventually it will cease to have value; it will cease to exist. Begin to wish for your wholeness, for your experience of Oneness, which is your natural condition, instead of wishing for something that is not real.

"The purpose of the body is to identify you in the made-up world. Having a body does not diminish or modify you as spirit in any way. Identifying solely with the body and forgetting that you are spirit is the problem. Spirit remains where it has always been. You have never stopped being spirit.

"You don't understand this because you cling to the belief that if you relinquish your hold on this limited identification of yourself, this body, then you will cease to exist. You also believe that death is possible. You believe that beyond this limited expression of yourself as a body, there is nothing else. You will not disappear! I am still here, am I not?

"The reason why you feel such tension in your body is that you are projecting all your remaining fear and self-loathing onto your body. It is a last-ditch attempt at clinging to your separateness. As you open yourself more and more to joining, this clinging grows fiercer. Persist as you have been doing. Dare to walk through it. You have mighty companions by your side. Let it happen, right here; there is nowhere to go. There is no need for further delay. Come and join your awakened brothers and sisters.

"Your fatigue comes from far too long a time spent pushing away the truth. Always the problem is resistance to experiencing the fullness of your Being, clinging to your littleness. That is very tiring. You are pushing away the Allness of eternity for the smallness of a lifetime. That requires a lot of effort; it is understandable that you feel tired. What you really feel is sick and tired of not being You, sick and tired of not being all that God is Being in you. What you are really tired of is not being your whole Self, awake.

"It takes great effort to be what you are not, to be less than your wholeness. You are toggling between moments of awakening and periods of falling back into ignorance. It is a period of adjustment. You still do not trust that full awakening is your divine birthright because you still do not fully accept your essential divinity. Continue to allow yourself to fall into it. The more you experience this, the more comfortable you will become with the complete allowing of Being. Do not attempt to reproduce what you felt yesterday or a week ago. Simply be open to reproducing the allowing. Since what God is Being at any moment is new, do not drag memories into the experience. Let it be new every time.

"Everything that is occurring is occurring in the Mind of God. Even your experience of yourself as a separated individuality is occurring in the One Mind because the One Mind is all there is. The problem is that you believe that what is occurring in your separate mind is occurring independently from the One Mind, that it is actually real. You guard and protect this separateness fiercely. The body, the physical experience, is really occurring in the mind. You have grabbed onto this physical experience as a way of delimiting yourself and marking yourself off as a separate individuality.

"Releasing hold of this identification of yourself as a separated individuality will not lead to the end of your existence, as you fear. This fear causes you to cling fiercely to your identification as a physical body. What is difficult for you to comprehend is that the physical experience is occurring in the mind. There is nothing outside of mind. Bodies do not exist outside of mind. There is no outside. This is a belief that is at the heart of the idea of duality.

"To say that there is something that should be ignored because it is not real or because it is an illusion is to say that there is something besides what God is Being. Whereas the truth is that there is nothing outside of God, so you experience either what God is Being or a misperception of what God is Being.

"The problem is your identification with form *alone*. You hold it in time and give it your definitions. Form in truth is not fixed. It is fluid and is constantly changing. However, as long as you hold it in time and give it your definitions, it loses its fluidity. There is an experience of form, yet form is not rigid. This is why the body can experience instantaneous healing. This is why it is possible to go from one place to another in an instant without the need of a vehicle. There is no limited or limiting physical matter, but there is an experience of form in an instant. If you let go of your idea of what things are, their true meaning will be revealed to you. As true meaning is revealed, form can change, as needed.

"You think there is a fixed order to your experience of yourself in a body, that you were born, that you started out as a baby and that the body grows old and gradually deteriorates. You believe that something that is of God can actually age, decay and die. This is your current belief, based on your learning and memories. Though you expect that life will unfold this way, it does not make it the truth. As long as you cling to this belief, this is the experience you will appear to have. If you were to abandon these beliefs, your experience of yourself as body and your experience of everything else in form would change. You would then be able to experience the beauty and wholeness of what God is Being in everything that you encounter every moment of every day; you would not experience any single thing as a limited form. Rather, you would experience the full meaning of what you encounter.

"The form of a thing simply gives it meaning. That's all. And in a moment, it is gone, because the next moment is new. There is no past and there is no history, and so there is no reason why you should expect that things would follow from your experience of yesterday or a year ago or decades ago. This seeming stream or sequence of the way things flow is based solely on your current limited view of the way things are. This is not the way things are in truth. The sooner you relinquish your own definitions, the sooner you will be able to appreciate the true order of Life, as God is Being it now. The body or the experience of form will no longer be a limitation to the full experience of the truth.

"There is a part of you that believes that you must *earn* your wholeness. This is why your healing is occurring in steps, in bits and pieces. It appears to be taking time. This is so you can measure your progress. You have earned it. You are practising letting go. You are practising leaning into the Father. You are practising looking for the more and expecting the more that is there for you. Part of you feels the need to measure this. *It is not necessary.* It is not true that you must earn your way to wholeness. But it is a belief that you still hold. When you no longer hold that belief, then the seeming progress or delay will cease, and healing will simply occur in its totality, which is the true state of your Being now, not in some distant future. Wholeness is for *now*. You do not need to work at, deserve or earn your wholeness. You only need to claim it and accept it *now*.

"Each person expresses God Being in a unique way. I know this flies against what you have learned along the way, where you believe that when you awaken, everyone comes together as one Son of God, but this is not accurate. God is eternally expressing in infinitely unique ways. Your healing is occurring in a way that is unique to you and expresses God's Divine Purpose for your wholeness. This is why each person's journey to awakening is unique. Each person must find that thread through the centre of their Being that leads them back to their wholeness. In your case, your healing is occurring as though in slow motion. It could have occurred instantaneously, but you are choosing to cling just a little while longer to your separate identity and separate will. This is only out of habit and also out of a lingering fear and lack of belief in your worthiness for awakening. You are so close, you cannot fail. You are on the threshold. Continue to let go, continue to trust, do not think, analyze, measure, evaluate, estimate or try to understand the process. Simply lean into the truth; trust the Father."

"It is true that you fear that letting go and letting God will lead to loss of control or chaos. But what you fear more is that you will lose the tiny freedoms you have gained for yourself and built into your life as a separate autonomous individual. You value these freedoms, in particular the freedom to think for yourself and to make your own decisions, more than you value waking up. You have understood that waking up requires letting God, or allowing God's Will to be manifest in you. Your true Self is what God is Being in you now.

"You fear that allowing yourself to be what God is Being in you will mean the end of your individuality. This is not true. You will maintain your individuality. The only difference is that your motivation will come from God, the Father, or doing God's work, or being what God has in Mind for you. This is where you get stuck. You do not trust that you will like this. The only way is to not think, and simply allow yourself to feel it more and more. Feel how it makes sense. Feel how it can only be a wonderful experience. Feel how total and complete freedom must feel better than your tiny little imagined freedoms and liberties.

"In a totally awakened state, you will have the freedom to be fully what God Wills for you. It is a far greater experience than can be offered by the separated individual running around with an identity that is limited to the physical body with a built-in life and death script. None of this is true. You are limited to a belief system that is untrue. Total freedom is experienced in the absence of limitations. Which sounds perfectly logical to you, yet you cling to limitations while saying that you cherish freedom. What you cherish is your tiny little freedoms, even if it means clinging to your limitations. This creates great inner tension and conflict. Release your belief in your limited self. Embrace the wholeness of what God is Being in you right now and trust that by letting go of your precious little freedoms you will encounter far greater freedom, the freedom to be all that God is Being in you. This is what awaits you. You are clinging to an unnatural condition in the face of the truth of who you are, and this causes tension, discomfort.

"Waking up does not require effort. The tension in your body is also a reflection of your attempting to make something happen, attempting to remove the blockages to awakening. It is far simpler than you think. Give up and allow it to happen naturally.

"Your awakening will happen in a way that is smooth, it will flow naturally. Nobody can make it happen for you. You determine how quickly or how slowly you wish to awaken. It cannot happen more quickly than you desire it to; it is happening on your schedule. This happens slowly because the person you think you are now will cease to be. If it were to occur too quickly, you would experience tremendous panic and fear over the loss of this self, the only self you know yourself to be at the moment.

"When mankind releases all the barriers to love, there will no longer be any need for the use of physicality as barriers, as frontiers and boundaries used for protection and separation. Your experience of physical matter is there because you refuse to accept love completely. It acts as a barrier against the full experience of love, which is an act of joining. This refusal to join or this rejection of love is at the heart of all the problems of humanity and the world.

"Trust that you can fully experience awakening and at the same time continue to function in the world. As you have begun to realize, this awakened state feels different from your normal state of ignorance. In your state of ignorance, you know yourself as the person with the personality that has been developed throughout the course of a lifetime. In your awakened state, that person and that personality have little or no bearing on what is occurring in the moment. Nonetheless, there is still a conscious awareness of what is occurring in the moment. You will not cease to exist. You will simply exist with a purer conscious awareness, one that is free of judgments and definitions from past learning. In this freer or purer conscious awareness, you are in a position to respond more fully to the needs of the moment in a way that is most appropriate. There is no need to try to sort through the past, to reason or to rationalize. Being is simple.

"Give up your long-held belief about who you are and what you are and lean into the Father so that what you are can be revealed. You might try this prayer:

"*I relinquish my long-held beliefs about who I am or what I am. I lean into the Father, trusting completely in His Love. I trust that I will be healed. I trust that my needs will be met. I relinquish all control and yield completely to the Father's Will.*"

Chapter 13

The Meaning of Love

The meaning of love is the meaning God gave to it. Give to it any meaning APART from His, and it is impossible to understand it. Every brother God loves as He loves you; neither less nor more. (ACIM.T.15)

I Will Always Love You, Until...

Special love relationships are a frequent topic of discussion during consultations with my clients. Yet, much of what passes for love— what is called "being in love" or even "making love"—seems to have little or nothing at all to do with love. More often than not, what is referred to as love is simply an assortment of agreements and bargains established between individuals. This kind of love says, I will meet your needs if you agree to meet mine. I will return your love as long as you meet my survival needs. I will support you if you do those things I want you to do. I will love you when you behave in a way that pleases me. You will be included in my intimate circle of friends if you agree with my perceptions and definitions of the world. More importantly, I will welcome you in my life and cherish you if you do not challenge my definitions of me.

In time, the loved one undergoes changes, perhaps grows more mature and self-respecting, has a "change of heart" concerning what is or what is not important in life, at which point old agreements no longer suit the new perspective. Alas, it appears that love has faded or altogether disappeared. Then begins the business of attempting to fix, repair, change or "upgrade" the outdated partner through means that can range anywhere from couple therapy to manipulation and coercion. Unless you change, I will withhold love from you. If these efforts are unsuccessful, the relationship ends and the search for a replacement love partner begins.

There is a tendency among spiritually minded individuals to become confused when their spouse or significant other does not embrace their quest. They see the inability to communicate or share what has become for them a very important subject as an indicator of a troubled relationship, as though the gift of love depended on the ability to discuss metaphysics or spirituality, or any other special subject for that matter. This outcome says that spirituality or the special interest is more important than acceptance—a key component of love. They have drifted apart, is a common conclusion, whereas, in truth, they have simply found a convenient way of placing a wedge between their hearts. It is said that the longest distance in the world is the distance between the head and the heart, and this is sometimes most evident with individuals engaged in a spiritual quest.

While discussing this subject with a client who was experiencing this very issue in her marriage, I asked her to recall that special feeling of snuggling up with her baby daughter after dressing her up in clean, fresh pyjamas. It felt great, of course, as any parent can attest. I asked if she would have considered withholding this love from her baby because she was not yet able to comprehend, let alone read, *A Course in Miracles*. Suddenly, the light went on and she saw her husband's disinterest in her spiritual path differently. It became clear that her work with the Course had been hijacked by the ego and used to push love away. In the end, what is important is not the study or the path, but the love that it inspires.

There is a collective call for change being expressed around the world today, as is evidenced by the growing number of postings on social media sites that reflect a deep yearning for an experience of something that is far greater and truer than the old familiar definitions of love. Whether it is a story about a mother cat nursing a brood of abandoned ducklings, a park ranger accepted in a pride of lions or a simple, random act of kindness, the message is the same: I love you *just because*. It is as though the heart of humankind is crying to be heard, seeking an experience of the love that is the essence of our Being.

Raj reminds us that love is the willingness to see what is there. To love is simply to give permission to a person or a thing to *be* what it is, just as it is. True love is frightening to the ego-identified individual because it can only exist in a state of defencelessness. Love follows the conscious act of letting down the boundaries of isolation. It is devoid of any self-serving investment, but, more than that, it does not depend on external circumstances or the behaviour of another. To desire an experience of love is to be willing to abandon all personal definitions and conceptions of what a person or thing is, for love is as new as what God is Being in the moment.

The Oppressiveness of Love's Opposite

While out on my daily walks, now and then my toothy smile or my friendly hello is met with a downward, uncomfortable expression. Not everyone wants to be acknowledged for the love that lies within. While the condo was being built, once or twice a week I'd drop by the office to chat with the condo representative. At the same time, I took pictures of the site as a way of being reassured that, although progress appeared slow, construction was actually moving forward. One time, as I was cutting across the train station on my way to the condo, I picked up an unusual message. Although I do not recall the exact words, the message clearly was that I should brace myself, which was surprising, since I enjoyed my visits with Condo Man. I always looked forward to hearing about the latest developments on the project and getting updates on the number of units sold.

No matter, I thought. I must have heard wrong. This time I had remembered to bring a paper with information about a page I had made on a social media website. I had set up a private group for condo residents, thinking it would be a great platform for sharing information about building maintenance and perhaps even decorating or shopping tips, and, of course, for getting to know each other. It was a simple tool for bringing people together and I saw only the upside. Excited to share my initiative, I showed Condo Man the tear sheet I had designed, punctuating my presentation with a list of wonderful benefits for residents, including the sharing of bulk purchases, especially handy for those trips to Costco. Apparently less enthusiastic than I was with the idea of using social media, Condo Man slammed it down before I finished listing the benefits. He wanted nothing to do with it, nor would he be presenting it to other condo owners. That was the end of that.

I shouldn't have been completely surprised by this response, given that I had previously witnessed some of his smallness of mind toward others, but I must admit that I was taken aback. Clearly, my little project had triggered some fear in Condo Man, perhaps the fear of joining with others, and this fear of joining looked very much like hatred. In that instant, though clearly out of proportion with the actual event and having really nothing to do with Condo Man, I felt myself slip through a tear in the fabric of the dark heart of mankind. In contrast to the growing number of experiences of love I had been blessed with over the previous months, this had to be among the most vivid experiences of hatred in my lifetime.

Now I understood the meaning of that cryptic earlier message. When I left the condo office that afternoon, I felt as though I had fallen completely out of grace. I scrambled to get back in touch with what was good, but the good was nowhere to be found. Instead, I felt myself drowning in a festering pool of hate. All of humanity's hatred washed over me in that one incident that should have been a non-incident. Unable to shake the stench of hatred from my being, I decided to go for another walk, this time in the opposite direction, where I would be able to connect in a more loving way with the people I met along the way.

As I made my way home that day, I reminded myself of the ever present nature of love. As the darkness dissipated, I saw snippets from my own life in which love had been either blocked or alto-gether withheld, especially in those times when I had expressed myself with childlike exuberance. In those days, children were to be seen and not heard. It became clear that I had accepted to believe that to express myself would not be rewarded with the love I desper-ately sought, and as long as I searched for love outside myself, my ego-based belief would be validated. Love was fragile, it could be taken away and withheld and any attempt to find love or to express love would be crushed. In order to survive within the framework of these beliefs, the only solution had been to withdraw into myself and to live in an impenetrable shell of self-protection.

As I continued on my walk, I joined with my friend and gradually the light returned. Once again, in the quiet stillness of my mind, I waited for whatever tidbits Jesus might send my way.

"To come from love—as opposed to judgment, separateness or differences—benefits you as well as the other person. To withhold love from anyone is to withhold love from yourself. If you feel that love has been taken away from you, damaged, pushed away or rejected, it is that you have decided that you are not worthy of love, that the Father is withholding love from *you*. This is obviously a lie, again, an ego distraction. Set it aside and remember that love cannot be taken from you. Whenever you accept this lie—that love is vulnerable, that you are vulnerable, that love can be withheld from you—this causes you to react by putting up defenses. This is what the ego wants. This serves the ego's purpose. Once you have established defensive walls or the need to defend yourself, separation has been reinforced. Love has more difficulty penetrating the stronger the walls of separation and differences are."

Since I had for many months been engaged in the practice of looking for the more that is there and opening my heart up to others in a less defended way, it was inevitable that I would encounter the deeply buried lies that acted as barriers to the reception and expression of this love. This was the journey through the centre of my Being, and so it was only natural that I would encounter my blockages. The fact that I had been so deeply disturbed by what was otherwise an insignificant encounter was an indication of just how close it had hit home. I knew that all that was required of me was to pay attention to the feeling, pay attention to what it was saying and listen for its meaning. And what it was saying is that I had for too long accepted that I was not worthy of love.

The Indestructibility of Love

It had been nearly six months since I had hosted a *Course in Miracles* meeting in my house. in transition between the house and the condo, much of my excess furniture had been sold, including the large futon that had served as a couch. And so it was that three of us found ourselves sitting on the floor with cushions and blankets in the small room that temporarily served as a yoga, meditation and television room. Also absent was an agenda or even a topic for the meeting. In fact, in the last year or so, most of our meetings had consisted of small gatherings of four or five friends who came together simply to share thoughts, feelings and experiences that reflected their individual journeys of awakening.

With just the three of us, the atmosphere was understandably casual but, above all, comfortable and safely intimate. It was the perfect environment for sharing and suitable for inviting in the light. This is what happened as the topic gravitated to personal relationships, families and childhood experiences, and each in turn shared freely, without judgment or condemnation, just peaceful sharing. The interesting thing about revelation is that you never know when it will occur. A foundation of mutual respect, unconditional love and acceptance is all that is needed for the seeds of healing to germinate. It was past midnight when it occurred to us that perhaps we might end our meeting. I went to bed that night pondering the patterns of my past experiences, the binding complexity of personal relationships and how they all wove together to make a solid case for the withholding of love not only toward others, but also toward ourselves. Upon waking the following morning, I had a very clear sense of the indestructible nature of love, a profound and unshakeable knowing deep in my *Being*. A heart can appear to be broken, stomped on, abandoned, humiliated and torn to shreds, but it cannot be destroyed. Love is the eternal substance of our essential Being and so it cannot be destroyed.

Individual Integrity in Personal Relationships

What do you do when you know you have come from your place
of integrity, from your heart, you know you have done the best you
could, yet your friend, family member, co-worker or partner—the
person with whom you are engaged in a relationship that requires
healing—responds with judgment or hate? This is a question I asked,
as did many of my clients.

"If you were coming from a place of integrity, from your heart,
you know that you were coming from the right place. Everyone
should always come from that place. When you come from this
place of innocence, which is from a place that is not motivated
by guilt, and the other person is not ready to accept their own
innocence, they feel uncomfortable. They can get upset, even mean
and vicious. This is simply because, from their perspective, they
are seeing something threatening. They are seeing another way of
seeing themselves, a way that is not filled with judgment, fear and
guilt, a way that comes from a place of innocence, something that
they have rejected for themselves. They are not ready to see themselves through the lens of love.

"The only thing you can do is to be aware of your own reaction.
Did you lose your sense of peace? Did you stray from your centre?
Did you doubt yourself? As you begin to practise respecting your
integrity, coming from your centred place, you can at times feel
uncertain. You will not always find confirmation that this is the
right thing to do, at least not outside yourself. Confirmation must
be found within, hence the importance of establishing a relationship
with guidance. If you are relying on the outside world to validate
your actions, you are looking in the wrong place. You are looking
for validation in a place where validation will not be forthcoming.
If you were looking for validation for guilt or ignorance, you would
have no problem finding that.

"Keep in mind that the condition of ignorance, in a world of
bodies, where there is the absence of total love, is maintained
by mutual agreement. As you begin to break away from that, for
example, when you respect your own integrity and decide that you

are not going to do the dance of guilt, then this agreement falls apart. There is a shifting, and this leads to temporary uncertainty. The ground on which you have previously stood seems to crumble beneath you. Do not allow this crumbling false ground to weaken your resolve to seek the truth. The truth is there, it has simply been hidden temporarily by the false ground on which you stand, a ground that is being maintained by your mutual agreement to be separate. As you stand your ground and persist in this movement toward enlightenment, you will be supported; but the willingness to move through the darkness into the light must come from you and it must be firm. When those conditions are met, confirmation and support will be there; you will not be left alone. It would be a delaying manoeuvre to indulge in doubt once you have made the decision to move in that direction. Do not waste time on doubt. Again, keep moving forward.

"You are never responsible for the reactions and responses of your brothers and sisters. You are responsible for allowing yourself to be from your centre, from your integrity. It is by being in that place that you set an example for others. In time, they will come to see that coming from their centre is better than coming from a place of darkness, guilt, anger or hatred. They will do this on their own schedule, when they feel comfortable. You need not worry about their process. Know that the love is there, in their own centre, in their wholeness, just as it is in you and in me. It simply waits for them to turn their attention toward it, as you have.

"When burdened with a situation involving another person that causes you to feel guilt, no matter the circumstances or the seeming guilt, you can try this exercise: Imagine being with the person in question and having a conversation from an entirely different point of view. Imagine speaking with this person from outside the dream, with both of you fully awakened. You may acknowledge that perhaps you agreed to come together in this dream to experience the circumstances that you did. But know that this was only for the purpose of promoting clearer awareness and eventually leading you to wonder if there might be more, if there might be a better way of looking and, ultimately, contributing to your awakening.

"Imagine the both of you smiling over the situation. See how silly the whole thing was, how unreal as seen from a broader, truer perspective, from Reality. You may start by sharing that you no longer wish to hold onto the guilt, the anxiety, the concern or the worry attached to the grievance. You can engage in this practise regardless of whether or not the other person is inclined to experience forgiveness and healing. In fact, this is an excellent way of addressing such a circumstance. You do not need to be speaking with a person face-to-face. If you are in the quiet place in your mind and invite them to join you in the quiet place in their right mind, you can communicate with them on that level. In fact, this is where you really join with a brother or sister.

"This does not mean that they will agree with you in the world of form and dreams, but you may assume that outside the dream they have heard and understood. When potential conflict arises, from that quiet place within, you can simply tell the other person that it is finished now. It is finished. We no longer have need for this. It is done. Choose peace instead. You can tell this to the other person, while addressing them in their right mind. It will help you in your defencelessness. It does not matter if the person is there or not. Always what matters is what is going on in your mind. If you are being defensive, you are not at peace and you are not in a position to awaken and see the more that is there in yourself and in your brother. If you are defenceless, you can see what is truly there. When thoughts of conflict in a relationship arise, you can always recall the conversation you had while in your quiet centres."

Tears of the Heart

Each time I walked to the condo, I passed by Mary Queen of Peace Church. Never having been much of a practising Catholic, normally, I would not have given it a second thought except that after a while, I began to sense a growing urge to connect with Mary, the mother of Jesus, the one who had played a significant role in his awakening by helping him remember his divinity. Mary came to mind more and more frequently until one day, in meditation, it occurred to me to ask if she might have been one of my guides. The answer that came was an unequivocal yes. And if I had any doubts, I was shown several instances of her loving presence in my life, a hand on my shoulder when only the end seemed a viable option, a loving presence when all seemed lost; and, as the scenes unfolded before me, I wept uncontrollably. While she had been waiting for me to turn my attention to her, instead, for most of my life, I had held an attitude of resentment toward women in general and, in particular, toward the fact of having been born in a female body. Great relief washed over me as I allowed this love to embrace me. From that moment, I made it a point to invite Mary into my presence when I did my yoga practice or whenever I felt tension in my body. Always, her loving presence was felt as soothing and enveloping. As I allowed this new love into my life, I began to allow myself to be a child again. This new allowing felt good, and many times the only response was to let the tears flow.

Not a crier by nature, I grew curious about my tearful bouts. Most of the time, I let the tears flow; unless I was about to walk into a public place and didn't want to be seen with puffy red eyes, in which case, I would take a deep breath and pull myself together. Most often, they were short bursts of tearfulness, like a sudden wrenching of the heart. In a way, they were silly, because afterwards I just wanted to laugh. These sudden outbursts would occur after having experienced a glimpse of the truth or an expression of love. I learned from clients that I was not the only one to experience tears when touched by love. In fact, I was growing accustomed to seeing the tears flow when we touched on love during consultation. I knew that these were not tears of sadness and that they were tears that came from the heart, but I remained curious to learn more about them.

"The tears you are experiencing are the tears of release of your Soul. The Soul is, if you want to call it so, the feeling organ of your Being. For most of your life, you have repressed this form of experiencing life. You have strengthened the thinking function over the feeling function. It is only natural that as you open up to what the Father is Being, as you relinquish control, as you give up the need to understand and simply let go and let God, a great relief is experienced. That will be felt by your Soul and that will be expressed as an outpouring of tears. No, they are not tears of sadness; they are in fact tears of profound joy. In fact, the joy is so profound that it is experienced as what you call gut-wrenching tears, but it is a very joyful experience."

I knew it was nothing I should be worried, concerned or alarmed about, and, increasingly, as I meditated, I allowed myself to fall into the Father. As I allowed myself to experience total and complete faith, as I became aware of the love and the support that is there, the tears would flow. And I knew that this was as it should be when one allows oneself to be fully enveloped in the Arms of the Father.

It Looks Like Love

There are countless books and teachings on the subject of love. We claim that love is the greatest healer and that it is the answer to all of the problems of the world. Yet, if love is all there is, if love is the only true worthwhile experience, then, Jesus, why do we continue to choose hate instead of love?

"When you have chosen for separation, you have abandoned love. So the choice for hate comes from the choice for separation, for seeing separate interests, for needing to protect and defend yourself from others, and to define yourself as different from others. This cannot lead to an experience of love since love is all-inclusive, love is defenceless, love comes from a place of peace, not fear. Love comes from a desire to see your brother as innocent.

"Because a person appears to have pushed away love, it does not follow that they have succeeded in pushing away love. Love cannot be destroyed or altered or pushed away. It can be ignored. You can always look for the love that is there instead of the fear of the love, which is really behind an act in which somebody would be pushing away love.

"If you see anything but love when you look upon your world, it is because you have first forgotten to turn to the quiet centre within, the altar of God, in your mind. If you had first looked within, you would have seen either an expression of love or, the only other alternative, a call for love. If you see your brother calling for love, it is only that he has forgotten, for a moment, that there is only love. Having yourself remembered the truth, you can gently remind him that he is loved by remembering yourself that there is only love.

"Always, the answer is the same: let love find its natural expression through you, for love is who you truly are. What is the Father Being? The Father is always Being love. No matter how well you obscure it, no matter how convincing is your perception of the contrary, the Father is always Being love. Love is welcoming and it does not judge. The Father's love is patient. Love must give of itself because it is its nature. It is expansive, broad and all-encompassing. It is therefore in constant movement. That is why in order to know love one must give love. This is its nature.

"Love is wise; it understands the situation and will always propose an appropriate solution. It is gentle, and never causes harm. Love is firm and unwavering; it is not subject to the laws of insanity. Love is given freely, and waits only to be accepted. Once accepted, love is complete."

A Course in Miracles says that it does not teach the meaning of love, for that is beyond what can be taught. This statement baffled me at first, but I came to understand that love does not need to be taught, much less earned or deserved. Love needs only be welcomed since it has always been the source of our Being and awaits only an invitation from us.

The wind had picked up and dark clouds loomed over the northern horizon and so I stepped up my pace a bit, but my state of peace remained unruffled. As I walked home from the grocery store, I remained aware of my surroundings, wanting to witness the Presence of God. If God and His Creation is all there is, then He must be here, now. I wanted to see the Kingdom of Heaven that is everywhere—that is *here*. God is in the gravel, the steel of the train tracks, the concrete of the sidewalk and the bricks of the newly renovated veterinary clinic I passed. God is in the air that I breathe. Will I see the Kingdom of Heaven one day? What will it look like? I pondered as I continued briskly. I let the question settle, without preconception, simply allowing the answer to come. What does the Kingdom of Heaven look like? I would like to see the Kingdom of Heaven. I think I am ready now. The answer was not long in coming, and in my quiet, peaceful state of mind, I was ready to listen and hear.

"There is only love. You will not see it with your physical eyes. You will know that you are in the Kingdom of Heaven by your experience of love. Love is all that there is to be experienced. Everything else is a substitute, a delay or a choice for ignorance. Love is whole and all encompassing, it is everywhere and it is for always.

"If you feel lack or need of any kind, know that you have attempted to make a substitute for love.

"If you are in pain, know that you are experiencing the discomfort of attempting to be anything but a child of God, wholly loved.

"If you are angry or upset for any reason, know that you have decided to push away love for a while.

"If you feel afraid, alone and abandoned, know that you have simply forgotten for a moment that you are forever loved by the Father."

Chapter 14

Trusting the Unfolding

God's Will for me is perfect happiness. (ACIM.W.101)

Don't Quit Your Day Job

It seems that while a spiritual pursuit should bring increased clarity about the nature of reality, when it comes to the practical stuff of everyday life, confusion and disorientation replace what was once straightforward. For many people on a spiritual path, the "day job" can become a subject of concern. Common questions and concerns include, what kind of job should I have now that I am a *Course in Miracles* student? My job is not very Zen and I think it is slowing my growth and my learning. I feel like withdrawing to a cave in Tibet, where it is quiet, less busy and less chaotic. It would be easier to practise my spirituality in a more harmonious environment. I'm busy practising forgiveness but the people around me don't appear to be changing. My co-workers aren't interested in learning about forgiveness; they seem to be quite content living with ego attitudes. How can I make them see that there is a better way of doing things? How can I make my workplace a more spiritual place?

I have found in working with thousands of clients that most people have allowed themselves to be guided toward a career or job that in some way reflects their innate skills and talents and therefore suits their Soul's growth. Clearly, this suggests the existence of an inner intelligence, a spirit that guides us through the small and great events of our lives. If a situation, job or career engages even just a few of a person's talents and abilities, chances are that they are in the best environment for their unfolding. Even in those times of overwhelming uncertainty, there is very often a sense of the presence of this guidance, a small voice that suggests what might be the right thing to do. Many of my consultations with clients serve little more than to confirm that their "inner voice" has pointed them in the appropriate direction.

There is no denying that in this fast-paced world, we constantly experience change, and *A Course in Miracles* is definitely about change; it's about changing one's mind and looking in a different way. This may entail some changes in your life, but these changes will come as a natural consequence of having changed your way of looking.

However, when beginning to work with a teaching such as the Course, it is easy to be tempted to make radical life changes. In such a case, it is likely that the ego has hijacked the process, since the ego does not like change unless it suits its purposes. The introduction of radical change may actually remove the very classroom needed for healing. While the change may be motivated by confusion and disorientation, what is actually happening is that the truth is beginning to register and the old way of seeing no longer makes sense. It is the ego that is disoriented. The simplest and quickest way Home is to apply your spiritual teaching in your familiar day-to-day life.

Major life changes generally require our full attention, which is also a great ego-inspired way of distracting us from the pursuit of awakening. There is one appropriate question to ask when feeling urged to make changes: What is the purpose of this change? When uncertain, doing nothing can be the appropriate response, at least until clarification occurs. When attention is focused on the quiet centre within, change will occur naturally, as it is needed. Since peace is the condition for awakening, that's not a bad place to focus our attention.

Jobs are associated with doing and most of us are adept at doing, but the Course says I need do nothing. This means that we need do nothing other than what our inherent nature expresses naturally. Once we awaken, we still need do nothing because then God's Will is being freely expressed through us. We have always been God's Expression, only we think we have the ability to make things happen. We think we need to struggle, overcome obstacles and prove ourselves. Yet, being sons and daughters of God, there is no need to prove anything; we only need to allow our perfection, our wholeness to be expressed. The ego constantly needs to validate its existence because it is not real; what is real does not need to justify itself. As we learn to trust in the wholeness that lies within, the true meaning of our life is revealed; as we yield to the truth of who we are, life flows with grace and purpose.

The Orderliness of Creation

When I was writing *Leaving the Desert,* I had planned to insert a chapter on numerology. But I didn't; instead, I set it aside. When I was writing my last book, *Choosing the Miracle*, I inserted the section in an appendix. Again, I pulled it out of manuscript before it went to print. I was concerned about the fact that numerology and astrology are part of the illusion and they shouldn't really work because they are magic. On the Internet, I had read comments from people who didn't believe in these tools and even suggested they should be overlooked by serious *Course in Miracles* students. Because my primary source of income was from my astrology-numerology practice, I needed clarification on this matter.

Furthermore, I wanted to know why I had chosen such an obscure career path. Being in a 9 year of endings, I wanted to know if I would be abandoning my practice and pursuing a different career path. Should I leave it for another, more normal career? As told in *Choosing the Miracle*, I had only half-jokingly considered getting a job in a flower shop nearby, until the morning I was very clearly advised that that was not going to happen. I received several bits of guidance on this important subject.

"Yes, the numbers [numerology] are part of the magic of this world, but they also bring you great joy. It would be like enjoying working in the garden and seeing the beauty of the flowers explode in the garden even while knowing that the physical garden is only a limited aspect of Reality. Anything that brings you joy brings you closer to God's Expression of who you are. They also have the additional benefit of bringing clarity to your brothers and sisters, again, bringing them and you closer to God's Expression. What does God want to express through them? If they are clearer in their expression, how can that be a bad thing? How can this form of magic be overlooked? There is nothing wrong with joy or clarity; they are part of God's Expression.

"You need to embrace the career path that you took many, many years ago—many lifetimes ago actually. Embrace it, trust it and accept that it is good. Know that you are helping people and, again, that is good. You can do good. Value the good work that you do instead of trying to attack it and demean it. That is your tendency. You beat yourself up, push yourself down and make what you do valueless, when what you do has tremendous value. Forget what some naysayers might say. If they are not comfortable with numerology, they can skip over those sections or move onto another book. Pursue your path, and in your path, you will find God's Expression, what God wants you to be.

"It is your great love of order that attracted you to the study of astrology and numerology. Because you have chosen to be ignorant about the orderliness of the universe by limiting your perception to the state of sleep, it does not mean that there is no orderliness in Creation. In fact, it is all orderly. God did not plan for your ignorance, but there is a plan for your joy and your complete unfoldment in the universe. You can use your astrology and numerology tools for this purpose.

"Structure and order are not bad. Order allows things to flow more smoothly. You do not need to create the order or modify it in any way. Simply allow the order that flows naturally from the Mind of God. Welcome it, make place for it and allow it.

"Do you wonder why there would be orderliness in Creation? If there were not order, then there would be chaos. Order facilitates the clear and beautiful expression of what God is Being. Chaos would render this expression more difficult to appreciate and even meaningless. Order is of God, disorder or chaos is of the ego, it is made up, therefore it can never be real or have any real impact or effects. If you wish to experience what God is Being or the order that God is expressing now, you must abandon your own interpretations, your own structure, the meanings that you have given to structure and order.

"If you allowed order to unfold the way it is meant to, there would not be any accidents on the road, you would find parking when you needed it, the light would turn green for you, and there would not be any impediments to your movement.

"In answer to your question as to whether or not you should change your career direction, the answer is no, not at this time."

Trusting the Flow of Change

Maybe a change of career was not on the horizon, but a major change of lifestyle was and I wasn't sure I was going to be comfortable with that much change. My friend Ken, a psychic, had tried repeatedly to get a hold of me through Skype, and when he finally did, it was to give me a warning about the condo. Don't sign anything and have a lawyer nearby was his message. Of course, this got me to worry some—a lot! I was just about to put my house up for sale and now there was a possibility that maybe I might not have a condo to move to. I tried very hard to remain at peace and leave everything in the Father's Hands, but there were moments when I couldn't help but feel uncomfortable. Being told that I should get in touch with a lawyer—just in case—got me more than a little rattled. I felt tense and uncomfortable, so I checked in with Jesus. As usual, though not always evident at first, he addressed the real cause of the problem.

"You are feeling the full contrast between the two ways of looking. The tension you feel comes from not choosing fully one or the other. It's time for you now to trust completely and choose for the Light. You will see the darkness fade away because it is not real. Let it go and trust. All will not disappear when you yield to the Light. On the contrary, everything that you truly are, everything that Is, will be there to be experienced in its Divine fullness.

"Let go of your limited experience. It is the clinging to these limitations that causes you to have a sense of darkness and impending loss. The only impending loss is the loss of the darkness or, in other words, the ego's hold on you. There is only one thing to let go of—the darkness. The limitations, your personal definitions of the world and of your experiences in this world are the only things that need to be relinquished. Clinging to this false experience of yourself, while at the same time becoming increasingly aware of the greater Truth of who you are, is what causes tension in your body and your mind. Clinging to this false idea of the world is what prevents you from seeing and fully experiencing the Truth.

"The act of letting go is a simple act. It does not require great understanding; it does not require understanding at all. It requires simply the willingness to consider that maybe you have been limiting yourself to a very small part of the experience of who you are as a Daughter of God. It is a tiny part of the whole you as the Eternal Life Principle is Being you in the moment. This is what lies in waiting. The fear, darkness, impending doom or gloom you are experiencing is the ego's fear of its own impending demise, which will be experienced when you choose the Light. In choosing the Light, the darkness disappears. You will not disappear, although the ego will. You have been making all the decisions in your life based on a self-made definition of yourself, of your world and of your life. Now you are facing the Truth of who you are, and this requires letting go completely of these old, limited definitions.

"This shift in Being, which is really a shift from your artificially made-up version of your Being to the true Being that God is Expressing in you right now, is what is causing you fear. There will only be fear if there is lack of trust. Foster your trust; build up your trust. Look for the evidence, as you have been witnessing, of the fulfilment of your Being through the very fact of your needs being met, in time, in an orderly fashion."

I understood that things were flowing in an orderly fashion, but I really would have liked to know how the sale of the house would proceed, how long it would take and then if the condo would be finished on time. I wanted Jesus to reassure me that all would go well, that I was not making a monumental mistake.

"I cannot tell you right now exactly what is going to happen, because I would be withholding from you an opportunity to strengthen that trust. If I told you that the condo would be ready on such-and-such a date and everything was going to be fine, you would stop worrying not because you were entrusting your life to the Father or to the unfolding of your Being, but because of what *I* told you. That would not be fair to you. I can help you by reminding you to trust into what is true, the truth of your Being, the truth of what God is Being. You want to awaken; you do not want to have a more comfortable sleep. Continue turning toward awakening, toward the Father, the altar within, the Light. Remain in that direction; keep your attention focused. To allow yourself to be distracted by what appears to be going on in form—a form that you have set up—is only a delaying manoeuvre.

"What causes you concern or anxiety or fear is being in a place of not knowing what is going to happen. This is actually a far better place than you realize. When you are confident that you know what is going to happen, you are deluded into thinking that you know what is going to happen in a dream you are imagining. By yourself, you cannot know what is going to happen in Reality. Since you are not the director of your eternal life, you can only *allow* what is going to happen. You are upset when unexpected situations arise in a false world in which you believe you have a plan. You become upset with change when you believe that you know where you are going and what your life purpose is. But all of these ideas are little more than threads in the story of a dream that you are maintaining.

"A part of your current anxiety comes from the fact that you feel the need to control the outcome when the fact is that you cannot know what is going to happen in the coming months. What causes stress is the tremendous burden of maintaining a false sense of security that is based on little more than the thread of a storyline in a dream. Let go of your storylines, your expectations for the future, your preconceived ideas, those dreams, those fantasies that give you a false sense of security. They are what feed fear and doubt. Your eternal Being cannot breed fear or doubt; nothing can happen to it. Let go of all your thoughts of what is to come and yield to the complete safety, abundance and fulfilment of what God is Being in you *now*. Your eternal Being is available to you *here*, *now*; it is not in some distant future. The idea of a future is illusory. In Being, there is no time. Being does not depend on what happened before or on what will happen in the future. Being is for *now*.

"All that you need is to be curious; welcome and embrace what God is Being in you. Give it a chance. Allow your Being to express itself; watch it, observe it and you will enjoy it. Set aside all of your ancient definitions of yourself. They are only definitions of a made-up, very miniscule self, an actor playing a role in a movie. Get out of the movie; pay attention to what your life is Being in every moment.

"You don't even need to think about what to do. All you need is to use your mind to pay attention. When you have lost yourself in your thinking, bring yourself back to the centre of your Being, to the mind that pays attention, and simply observe. Allow your Being to come through, to be expressed. Engage your curiosity and wonder about what is coming next. That is what it means to be like a child. What is going to *be* can only meet your needs; your fulfilment is what is going to *be*. Your own definitions, your own ideas, will not influence your fulfilment; they will only engage the limited views that you have of life and of yourself. Your Life is not yours to determine; your Life is not even yours to navigate. Your Life is yours to welcome and wonder about and allow. You are essentially not the boss of your life; the Father is. The Father being eternal— the Father being Love—can only bring what is eternal and what is good for you.

"Give up the habit of thinking. Practise silent allowing. Then you can pay attention to all that is Being without the limitations and the interference of your personal definitions."

Standing at the Door

Despite repeated guidance on the subject, I continued to experience pain in my back and left arm, especially when I got up in the morning. Somehow, this was an issue I was not ready to relinquish. I practised stretching exercises, but continued to feel tightness and pain in my muscles and joints. I asked my friend for help with this chronic condition.

"You still believe that you are not worthy of awakening to the fullness of your Being or to your full healing. You still harbour some guilt. However, this does not mean that you have to ferret out all the dark little bits of guilt that remain. Simply know that this is what is holding you back, and turn your attention back inward, as you have been doing, toward the altar. There's nothing wrong with taking some pain medication, and don't forget your homeopathic granules. Yes, they are magic, but at the same time, accept that you still believe that you are a body, also a form of magic.

"It's okay to take some pain medication, but beware that the absence of pain can draw you away from the altar within. The pain is motivating you to find healing. You know now that complete healing is available to you, and, in fact, your awakening is very near. You are standing at the door—each one of you is standing at the door—and you know that the door is open. You do not need to do anything special to pass through the door. You only need to trust. However, although this is entirely unnecessary, it is usually only when you experience difficulty or pain that you are motivated to find another way and consider passing through the doorway. In doing so, you will forever leave behind the dream of illusions and embrace your wholeness, your perfection as God created you.

"This new way requires abandoning everything you have learned about life and about yourself. This requires faith because you do not have guarantees of your perfection other than those made by a teaching such as *A Course in Miracles*. At the present time, you have few examples and few tangible experiences of what this will mean. This is why you are companioned on this journey; this is why joining is so important.

"The Course invites you to seek only the experience; do not let theology delay you. This might also have read, 'Do not let analysis, study, thinking, comparing and, above all, the need for understanding delay you.' To seek only the experience means to turn your attention to the altar within and stay focused on that. Continue to be inquisitive. Continue to want to experience the Truth. Continue to want to know what God is Being. Forget the guilt, know that you are worthy as a Daughter of God. It is your Divine birthright to experience the fullness of your Being."

Plying My Craft

November was fast approaching, which meant it was time to prepare to put the house on the market. Using my astrological knowledge, I decided to find the best date and time for this event. Electional charts are a time consuming activity because dozens of charts need to calculated and evaluated, but I felt it was worth the effort. At first, I hesitated as to whether or not I should bother with this technique, but I concluded that even if the world as I perceived it was an illusion, there was order in life. Astrology charts were just a reflection of that orderliness. Besides, this technique had worked well for my clients; now it was my turn. The parameters for my electional chart centred on a quick sale, harmony between buyer and seller, and a hassle-free financial transaction. The best date I could find was at the end of November, still a bit early for a spring sale, but the holidays would pass quickly and we would be heading into peak selling time.

While waiting for the sale date, I immersed myself in user guides, offers to purchase and counter-offers—and this in both English and French, French being the most difficult for me to understand—and as much related material as I could absorb. The trickiest part was establishing a selling price. I had a net price in mind that I felt was fair and met my needs. I was familiar with the neighbourhood, having lived there for over fifteen years, and had done a thorough market analysis.

At the end of November, at the elected date and time, I logged onto the Internet and activated my real estate profile. The house was officially for sale. The following day, I woke up feeling much less pain in my body. I felt as though I was standing on the threshold of being reborn, but this time I was being born into a vast unknown. There was only one thing to do—yield to the flow of the movement of my Being. Anything else would stir up doubt, anxiety and fear, all of which I no longer wished to experience. I longed for the Love of the Father and so I would pay attention only to that. That was my sincere, heartfelt desire. My friend endorsed my position with some positive feedback.

"You can approach the unfoldment of your Being as an adventure. Be curious, trusting that your unfolding will be comfortable and natural as it is sustained by the Father. Enjoy the adventure.

"To allow the unfolding of your Being is the easiest thing in the world to do. Simply allow it. This is why you need do nothing. Your perfect unfoldment is God's Will. As you withdraw your limited ideas and false definitions of who and what you are, what is Real will emerge. Your unfolding is occurring whether you are aware of it or not. To try to make up a life for yourself or to define yourself or your unfolding is like trying to catch the flow of water from the spout with your hands. This can only be a tiring and fruitless preoccupation. Instead, pay attention and enjoy the wonder of what the Eternal Life Principle is Being through you."

Deception

In early December, I visited the condo office for an update on the delivery date. The house was now officially listed, and I was wondering what move-in date I should give potential buyers. During that brief visit, I was very disappointed to learn that my move-in date had been delayed another month. I also learned that the slight modification to the floor plan I had requested, along with a couple of simple updates and additions, had been denied. It had been okay for them to make promises of options and floor colours and cabinetry before I signed my offer to purchase, but now these options had been reduced to a very few. In fact, the bathroom had only one option, which meant no choice at all, and it was a design I didn't like. All of this was fodder for the ego frenzy I found myself spinning into. I felt that I had been deceived. In fact, from what I was learning, it seemed the entire real estate industry was filled with lying, deceitful individuals, as were bankers, large corporations and politicians. In fact, the whole world was one endless pit of deception.

This line of thought had spun me out of my state of peace and in the quiet of the early morning hours, I listened for my friend's advice.

"Stop thinking," he said, and I knew he was smiling. In fact, I felt he was having a bit of a laugh at my expense.

Okay. I'll stop thinking.

"Instead," he continued, "look for the feeling behind the thoughts."

And I did, and I saw right away the fear that was driving this mental meltdown.

"You know that you are the one experiencing deception of a self-made nature. If you believe that the world has anything that you value, you are deceiving yourself. If you place your trust in the people and the things of the world, you are deceiving yourself. If you are seeing deception, it is your own self-deception that you are perceiving, and understandably, this makes you upset; rather, this makes the ego-identified part of you upset. You have been increasingly engaging in the practice of placing your trust in the Father, and this was bound to have an impact."

I went for my morning walk that day with my recorder in hand. I walked with a peaceful mind and listened for more guidance.

"This additional delay gives you a little extra time to fully make your commitment to your awakening. You will continue to toggle between the two allegiances a while longer, one to the Father and the other to your self as a separate individual. This extra time gives you the opportunity to experience first-hand what happens when you yield to the Father, when you trust completely the Will of the Father. To go any faster would deprive you of an opportunity to make this integration complete."

I had to agree with going slowly. Every step of the way I was feeling that I was at the edge of what I could handle. I had more in common with life in a cave in Tibet than life in the city. But if this was going to be an opportunity to practise strengthening my devotion to accepting the Will of the Father, then I was more than willing to suck it up and face the challenge knowing that the challenge was simply one of breaking habits and letting go of my allegiance to this limited perception of life.

"Know that it does not have to take six or seven months for you to come to the full awareness of your Divinity. It does not have to take any time at all. However, as long as you continue to harbour guilt and feelings of unworthiness, fear will arise and send you into a dark tailspin. This is what you have been experiencing lately. It's okay to take your time and go at a comfortable pace. There is no need to push or hurry because you know that the outcome is sure. Simply relax into it. Enjoy the unfolding of your Being. Let it happen, as it is already happening without any effort on your part."

Fear of Awakening

I began to suspect that a lot of the fear and discomfort about being in the world was coming from the fact that I was occasionally experiencing glimpses of spirit. Spirit was so different, so much more awesome than the limited perception of the dream. I was growing increasingly curious about the possibility of one day—note that I purposefully ignored the six or seven months that Jesus alluded to—experiencing full awakening. What happens to everything you have known about yourself, about your life?

"You are afraid that by letting in the true light, it will obscure everything that you are familiar with, everything you are accustomed to seeing with your physical eyes. That is not true. Awakening will allow you to see more of what is there   all of what has been previously obscured by your limited vision. You are also afraid that you are moving to a space that will feel confining. You have the illusion that the physical space around you in your current living arrangement gives you the feeling of spaciousness and freedom that your spirit seeks. That is not true. You could feel completely free in a closet.

"You will be fully awakened when you will have given up any remaining interest in the limited world. You will not lose your memories; however, you will not use them to make decisions. When you use your memories to make decisions, you are keeping away the newness of what God is Being in the moment. It is a form of control, and control is a way of dealing with fear. You are afraid to trust and allow what God is Being without relying on your own control and memory. In a fully awakened state, inspiration arises and appropriate action will be expressed."

If I use memory and past learning in any way, then I am keeping away the truth. The truth comes from that quiet place of peace in the mind and it is what God is Being now. It is going to be something new. In the same way, if I cling to desires and expectations for the future, I will not be available to experience the truth of what is unfolding in the present moment.

"You move gradually toward your awakened state because if you were to snap into it instantly you would feel lost, disconnected. Your awakened state is You, in the full awareness of your full Being; it is not somebody or something else. If you were to snap into it instantly, you could lose the connection with who you thought you were before you awakened. This is why the pace is gradual and in harmony with your level of comfort. Your memories will still be there but they will not carry the emotional charge that they had before.

"As you begin to welcome your greater awareness, as you begin to see that this can and will be a joyful experience, then you can gradually let go of your previous limited awareness. The broader awareness gradually replaces the limited awareness. The transition then is a smooth one, one that is more easily welcomed, and so the transition goes much faster that way.

"The more curious you are about experiencing the greater awareness, the less fear you will have, the faster will be your awakening and the sooner you will experience your full awareness. There is no reason why you should not experience this full awareness, or your awakening, at this moment. Other than your fear of losing yourself completely, as you realize that you no longer want to cling to a limited version of yourself, you will gladly relinquish your definitions. What you truly are as God created you will come forth and unfold and your Being will emerge.

"In a way, the time it takes for your awakening is proportional to the value you place in your limited self. The experience of awakening is an experience of broader awareness. In the awakened state, you have access to knowledge that goes beyond any knowledge that you can obtain as a separated, limited self. In an awakened state, you are joined with all that is there and therefore you have the knowledge of what is going on in the All that is there.

"To awaken does not mean that you lose your limited awareness. To awaken means that you lose the limitations to your awareness. Because what is beyond your limited experience is beyond your control, you need to trust that what is beyond is good, is whole, is loving and is God. The ego would have you believe that what is beyond your field of control is something dark, frightening and dangerous.

"The only thing that keeps you from experiencing the Christ in your brother is your desire to cling to your own definitions and understanding of what is here. To see the Christ in your brother is to experience God in your brother, it is to experience what God is Being. In order to do that, you must relinquish the limiting definitions you have given to that brother. This is the only way that you can truly experience what is truly here. To relinquish your own ideas and perceptions leaves you in a place of not knowing. This is a frightening place for a separate self whose identity is fully made up. You will no longer be able to make up definitions or give definitions to what is Being in the moment.

"On the other hand, you will be relieved of the *need* to make up definitions of what you are experiencing in the moment. That which you are experiencing will reveal its meaning to you, whether it be a flower or a brother/sister. Ask yourself what you really want: Peace? Wholeness? Truth? If this is what you really want, then you must look elsewhere than in a world of dreams and illusions where truth is not found. You must turn your attention inward to where truth is found. If truth is eternal, then it must be here, now; it must be readily found. If you do not see the truth, it is because you prefer to see something else in its place."

To continue on this journey would require total trust. It was made clear to me that I would have very little support in the world or from people who still believed that they were bodies. However, I would have total support from our brothers and sisters who are awake, who will be there for me. The one thing that would help guide and keep me on track would be the love being shared. Love is felt; if I turned within and took the hands of the ones who are helping us, I would feel the love. I needed to remind myself that I *was* loved, right now, not for anything I was going to do in the future or had done or not done in the past, but simply because I always had been and always would be loved. That would be my lighthouse, my guardrail. And yes, I knew that this was a totally unknown experience, but I was ready and I wanted nothing more than to walk into it.

"What happens when you abandon yourself to the Will of the Father?" I asked my friend while out for our daily walk.

"You find a place."

"Why?"

"You will be moved in a direction that is appropriate."

"Why?"

"Because you are loved and there is a place for all of God's children."

That sounds good. I would like that very much.

Chapter 15

Letting Go

The Soul never loses its communion with God. (ACIM.T.1)

First Offer

The morning after I put the house up for sale, I found my For Sale sign buried under an inch of snow. As it turned out, the installation kit had been missing a set of washers and the heavy wet snow pulled the sign right off the post. It was cold out and, with an early start to winter, this meant a late start for the real estate market. I secured the sign as best I could while awaiting a new kit, but then realized that it had been planted too close to the street. Yes, it was visible to passersby, but soon it would become buried underneath the mountain of snow. Two weeks later, after several passes of the snow removal crew, the sign was invisible. Luckily, a friend who lived nearby had an old wrought iron frame designed specifically for this purpose. I planted a new sign closer to the house. Another problem solved.

As a relatively private person, I might have felt uncomfortable with the idea of walking strangers through my house, but I didn't. I surrounded the property with love, gave it to the Father and trusted that the right people would find my house and all would proceed smoothly. Emails and phone calls began to trickle in, bringing potential buyers. Everyone who visited the house was polite, discreet and altogether very nice. A PowerPoint slide show was set up on the laptop in the kitchen to show potential buyers the splendour of the garden in the summertime. Just before walking out the door, one man paused and expressed how good it felt in the house. I smiled, thinking, yes, that's how love feels.

While any concerns I may have had about showing the house to strangers were quickly dispelled, such was not the case when it came to dealing with those in the real estate profession. I think I had more calls and emails from brokers than I did from actual potential buyers. Since this was my first house sale and I was eager to learn—but, mostly, since I was naive and unsuspecting—I agreed to meet with several of them. I soon discovered that they would say anything to obtain my listing, using all manner of scare tactics, promising disaster and even possible assault from dangerous visitors. It seems that the introduction of commission-free services in the marketplace had severely compromised their business and many of them took it upon themselves to fight for what they believed was their right, which was to plant their own sign on my lawn. Clearly, the real estate industry needed a makeover, but it was not my place to make the changes that would allow their industry to shift and grow with market trends. Frankly, I found it outrageous to pay five to seven percent commission on the sale of a property such as mine that might not require much more than ten to fifteen hours of work, and so not one managed to convince me to sign with them.

Barely three weeks later—actually, it was the day before the supposed "2012 end of the world"—I received my first offer. This was my first official interaction with an agent. He was aware that the house was listed with a commission-free service and he assured me that he would not be charging me his commission. His clients were a young couple who were looking to start a family; her parents lived a block away, and so they were familiar with the neighbourhood, appreciated its value and were very much interested. When they visited the house, they seemed to like it very much.

Before presenting the offer, the agent assured me at least three times that it really wasn't about the money, that normally he would not be taking on a listing in this neighbourhood, but these were nice young people and he was doing them favour. Then he showed me the amount on the cover page, adding that this was not the final offer. Although it was clearly not acceptable, for my own edification, I let him continue. He went through the document explaining the conditions of the offer, and when he reached the last page, he pointed out the actual amount I would be receiving, greatly reduced by his generous commission. It was mid-morning, and they were giving me until eleven o'clock that night to respond to the offer.

I was polite, even friendly, as I showed him to the door, assuring him that I would look at the offer and get back to him. Afternoon rolled into evening; at nine o'clock, I was on the phone and I noticed his name on the caller ID. I ignored the call. At ten, I decided to send him an email. I thanked him very much for the time he had spent with me that morning, pointing out that it had been a very enlightening experience. Then I politely declined their promise to purchase. At that price, I wrote, I preferred to keep the house.

He replied shortly after, asking if I would like to make a counter-offer. Given the sizable gap between asking and offering prices, I replied, I didn't think we could ever meet in the middle. But he persisted, asking if we could speak and look at other options. Although I did not see what other options there were, I agreed to speak with him the following morning, one of the busiest days of the year for me. It was Christmas dinner with my daughters and friends; I had a full day of consultations and, of course, hours of kitchen duty ahead of me. I was feeling borderline overwhelmed when I went to bed that night and I wasn't sure how to respond to the broker. Because those in the real estate business had lost their centres, it did not mean that I should be looking with the eyes of the ego. In my prayers that night, I asked for clarity.

When I woke up the next morning, I felt surprisingly very refreshed, calm and jovial. I thought about the offer and laughed. It wasn't a derisive laughter; it was simply the only appropriate response given the circumstances. When the agent called, I listened to his proposals, and then wrapped it up by apologizing for having misunderstood when he said that it wasn't about the money. I shared that I too engaged in occasional pro bono work, and so I thought he was waiving his fee for this young couple. I thanked him again for his efforts, and that was pretty much the end of our negotiation.

Over the holidays, I received more emails and phone calls from realtors, each one trying to convince me that I would do much better with their help. All the while, my brother, who loved the business of business and seemed to be particularly animated by my real estate adventure, coached me in his inimitably zealous, perhaps overly vigorous, style. It was almost as though he had made it his mission to ensure that I understood just how horrible the real estate business was. From guidance, I understood that he was just looking after my best interests; and the realtors, well, they were just doing their jobs.

As much as I wanted to see the Christ in everyone, I had to admit that my brother was right, at least in part, even in large part. It was very difficult to deal with individuals whose holiness was covered up by their assholiness. It got to a point where, whenever the phone rang, I cringed. Following a particularly unpleasant encounter with a pair of realtors who had tried to get me to sign their contract after keeping me hostage until well past dinnertime, I began to doubt that I had made the right decision to use a commission-free service. I even began to doubt that I had made the right decision to move. I could forfeit my deposit on the condo and stay in this house for the rest of my days. Let someone else deal with the sale.

The next offer I received is not worth mentioning and fortunately was made over the phone, wasting less time. I began to have bouts of fear and panic; condo delivery had been delayed another month, something horrible could happen to the house, I could lose everything. Clearly, the ego was having a field day. I noticed how easy it was to become distracted with the things of the world, and the more I allowed this to occur, the further and further I felt from my centre.

I lamented my monastic past, imagining how much simpler life would have been as a Tibetan monk. I would have been quite content to make lentil soup for my fellow monks for the rest of my days. But at the same time, I could see how a sheltered life would not have given me as many opportunities for shaking myself out of the comfortable stupor of life in a dream. Sometimes, we need to be prodded a bit, lest we never wake up. If there was one thing that could grate on me and push me to want to awaken and experience something other than my limited view of Life, it was quite rightly this real estate business. I was a fish out of water; I'd have to find a way to breathe. *God is the air that I breathe*, I reminded myself over and over and over. *God is the air that I breathe.*

A third offer came in early January, this time from a very nice agent, polite, respectful of my choice of real estate service. He explained that the commission would be paid by the young couple, or, more precisely, their fathers. They wanted to start a family, and this was the ideal neighbourhood for them. He worked very hard to sell the house to these young people, spending more than an hour going through the rooms, discussing options and possible renovations to make the house just right for them. The main concern for the young woman was that there was no walk-in closet and she didn't know where she would put all her shoes. I thought of my worn sandals and one pair of walking shoes and wondered what I might be missing in life.

They came for a second visit with their fathers, and the next day made an offer. This offer was much more reasonable, but the agent knew that it still fell short of the price I had in mind. Before making the presentation, he actually appealed to my sense of compassion by pointing out that this was a young couple, they were just starting out, the parents were not that wealthy and this would give them a chance to start their family. Again, I doubted my asking price, as well as my decision to sell without a broker. Again, I received more coaching from my enthusiastic brother, who gave me another pep talk on how to deal with agents. And, of course, it was pointed out that I could help my daughters—and *myself!*—before helping out a couple of strangers. I had done my homework, the pricing was good—the agents had actually told me so—and so I would stick to it. If I needed to change anything, I would be guided accordingly, but not by agents or anybody else with a vested interest in the sale of the house.

Okay, I concluded, this had been a great learning experience, but I had other business to attend to and the novelty had worn off. It was time to sell this house. I turned to my astrology program and searched out the best date for an open house. There was a very good date in February, during the waxing moon and just before Mercury turned retrograde. To put it off until the next suitable time would be cutting it close to my move-in date; I didn't want the stress. It was time to move forward.

The Unfolding of Being

The *unfolding of your Being is occurring with or without your aware-ness or your participation.* I thought about this statement a lot while my life was coming undone. As much as I would have liked to have been told with absolute certainty how and when I would sell the house, that the condo would be finished on time, that I would love it and everything would be fine, I understood that I needed to practise trust. What else could I do? While my life was unfolding at a pace that I found to be a little bit fast, I was curious about the outcome. If the unfolding of my Being was occurring no matter what, it meant that all of the events and situations and circumstances of my life had occurred regardless, or more accurately, in spite of my efforts to control, manipulate and make things move in the direction that I desired. Life was moving in the direction that it needed to move.

I continued to check in with Jesus when I could find time for a walk, and, as usual, instead of addressing my perceived problems, he continued to point me in the right direction.

"Now you can stand back and observe this unfolding with greater awareness. You do not need to interfere with it, just like your metaphor of the rose. [I sometimes pointed out to clients that life unfolded just like the rose, petal by petal, until it shared with the world its full beauty. Never would we consider interfering with this unfolding by pulling on the petals. Instead, we patiently watch, marvel and appreciate its beauty.] By simply standing back, observing and allowing, your experience will be far more fulfilling and rewarding. You will know with absolute certainty that there is a God, a Primary Source, and that no amount of meddling and control on your part can change this unfolding. All you need is to wonder and be curious and watch it happen. If you do not get in the way of the unfolding, it will occur smoothly, graciously, gracefully. There is no need for your unfolding to be a painful or even mildly uncomfortable experience. It should be an experience of awe, an experience of observing what the Father is Being in you.

"True joy does not come from having an outcome that you desire, for such an outcome can change or be taken away, which would mean that your joy would also be taken away. So joy is not dependent on a particular outcome. True joy comes from not holding onto any idea of what an outcome should be. It comes from watching without preconceptions and experiencing the unfolding of what God is Being. Individual will has nothing to do with this unfolding and your true joy comes from letting go of your personal will and desire to have outcomes that you choose.

"And, of course, when you start thinking rightly, naturally you are going to begin to experience things rightly, in the right way, as they are meant to be experienced. Your awakening to the fullness of your Being will never require you to do anything that is beyond your means or capabilities. Awakening is practical, gentle and intelligent."

In Saturn's Shadow

Astrologers use the orbit of Saturn, lasting almost thirty years, to mark the timing of significant turning points in life. The previous fall, I had had my second Saturn return. In astrology, each planet is ascribed a set of unique characteristics that describe its function in the human experience. Saturn has traditionally been associated with limitation, austerity, scarcity, darkness, depression, sadness—in effect, all that is contrary to the experience of joy and lightness of Being. Its prominent placement in my chart is a clear indicator of the culture of austerity and self-denial that darkened my existence for the greater part of my life. In fact, I had grown quite fond, even proud, of being able to live comfortably on a shoestring budget, buying only what I needed, avoiding eating out at restaurants and not wasting money on frivolous things like vacations, movies and whatever else people did for fun. It was this culture of efficient scarcity that I was confronted with when Saturn came around for its second return visit.

My new awareness of the fullness of Being that awaits us, each and every one of us—including me—came with the realization that God wants joy for His children, all His children, even me. He wants abundance, fulfilment and far more than the mere meeting of basic needs for all His children, even me—and you, too! It must be so, because God is Love, and He would not withhold anything from any of His sons and daughters. The Infinite Life that is the Source of our existence, the Cause of our Being, cannot be limited. Scarcity or lack of any kind can only be something that we are imagining while we are temporarily experiencing ourselves as separate from our Source.

I had been pondering the possibilities of this new perspective, feeling increasingly safe and protected, increasingly curious about what the Father might have in store for me, if only I allowed Him fully into my life. It was a Saturday morning in early February, and I had planned on checking out a small foldable ottoman that was on sale at Canadian Tire. A light coat of fresh snow covered the ground and I debated whether I should walk the two and a half kilometres or take the car. I had planned on taking the car, but the snow caused me to reconsider. It was very cold and the road would be slippery. I turned to the quiet place within and asked, should I walk or drive?

"You are making a decision based on fear," my friend pointed out. I think he liked shopping more than I did.

Yes, I was coming from fear, I conceded. And so I set the fear aside, got dressed and warmed up the car. I ran several errands that morning, thoroughly enjoying the interactions with my brothers and sisters along the way. When I arrived home, I thought about my fear of driving; clearly, it was beginning to cramp my style. In fact, it was turning me into a veritable recluse or perhaps it was just another means for validating my reclusive nature.

Again, from that quiet place in my mind, I heard clearly, "It's not the driving that's the problem, it's the car."

Yes, that was true. I did once love to drive. What I didn't like was the ABS system combined with the manual transmission; small patches of ice had sent me skidding on more than one occasion, scaring me half to death—no gears, no control, just a skid off to the side of the road. Then, of course, there was summer driving, which had become an obstacle course through never-ending construction zones—not fun when you're clutching and shifting all the way. Selling the car and using public transportation made sense, given the amount of driving I did. From where I lived, I ran many errands on foot, and I loved to walk. I saw myself enjoying the simple life, tucked away in my new condo, safe from the dangers of an increasingly noisy and busy world. If the cave in Tibet was not a viable option, I would make my own cave, in my condo.

Apparently, this is not what the Father had in Mind for me. My deeply engrained attraction for the monastic lifestyle was going to be laid to rest, once and for all. When I went for a walk that Saturday afternoon—the weekday that takes its name from Saturn—I felt strongly guided to veer off my usual route and make a detour to the Kia dealership. I wanted to look at a car that had recently caught my eye. I was just going to look, get a feel for what I could get for my car.

The dealership had a great deal on a cute compact, no interest for 60 months. I sat with a salesman and looked at the options. Again, I found myself over my head in business, money, financing and negotiation. While he worked on an amount for my trade-in, I walked around the showroom, examining other models, until I found the one I really liked, the one that had caught my eye when I first saw it on the road. It was more expensive and didn't have the same deal, but I really liked it. It was the one I wanted.

The following day, a friend I hadn't spoken with in a few months called. We caught up, and when I told her about my visit to the dealership, she recommended I enlist the help of a friend of hers, an expert in car shopping. Monday, I visited the dealership with Ernie, and while he negotiated the trade-in and sale price on my behalf, I revisited the car I liked. When I stepped out of the car to join the others, my friend chimed in, very clearly.

"Get the one you like."

I turned around, looked at the car I was walking away from, and shook my head. But it was more expensive.

My friend persisted. "Really, get the one you like."

Although this flew against everything I held to be fiscally reasonable, I enquired about the car I liked. I'm not sure exactly how it all happened, only that things flowed with great ease. My brother made a suggestion about how I could carry the cost until the house was sold, money was moved around, a very fair offer was made on my Saturn, thanks to Ernie—much better than I would have gotten on my own—and a good deal on the car I wanted was on the table. A week later, I traded in my Saturn—yes, I drove a Saturn—and drove happily off the lot in my new Soul. Yes, there is a Kia model called Soul. Go figure.

This episode with the car made me acutely aware of my unhealthy attitude toward my own abundance. I had developed a very neat and effective culture of financial efficiency, living well with very little, like the proverbial church mouse. I think I may even have raised managing scarcity to an art of sorts. I had made all sorts of purchasing choices based on this outlook, always buying on sale, buying cheap, buying no-name brands, lesser brands, avoiding organic. I made significant purchases by buying my second choice rather than my first choice for the sake of saving money. I had grown to dislike shopping—most likely because I never had any spare money to shop with. I was a famine shopper, buying when on sale and then stocking up. I had become a poster child for smart shopping.

Note that there is nothing wrong with smart shopping. However, this mentality of smallness and individual insignificance reflected a deeper ego sense; it is what kept me from becoming fully what the Father wanted me to be. It was guaranteed to ensure that I would not awaken, and to ensure that I would not fully embrace my Self as the child of God that I truly am. Smallness and God did not go hand in hand; Allness and God did. Poverty, as it is experienced in the world, is not a necessary part of the human equation. It is a mindset. I was beginning to see that we have as much abundance as we will allow. Since our abundance comes from our Eternal Life Source, to experience anything less than complete abundance is to deny ourselves our birthright.

The Wonder of Life

After the start of the New Year, a 1 Year of new beginnings, I began to feel as though a giant cosmic foot was pressing into my back, pushing me out into the world, propelling me forward to embrace life fully. Looking back, I saw how, from the moment I was born, I had tried to backpedal my way out of this life. My old patterns of thinking needed to be broken, and for that I needed to trust completely the movement of the unfolding of my Being. It was time to let go of my monkish mentality. If I had been meant to be a monk, I would have been born much closer to the caves of Tibet. I needed to embrace the place, the people, the movement, the noise and the life that was all around me because all of it was God's Expression.

On Valentine's Day, my friend Pooran left a message on my answering machine wishing me a happy day. But I was already bursting with joy and, actually, I couldn't have been happier, I thought, when I returned her call. "I've cracked," I said excitedly. Poor Pooran. I think she thought something bad had happened.

"No, I mean I've cracked, all my old stuff, my old patterns. I'm ready to live," I said to reassure her. While I used to think that somehow, one day, we wake up and leave, now I realized that we wake up and *live*. Something happened that day; I'm not sure how or what or why. All I know is that I felt free; the shell of self-protection, isolation, austerity and limitation that had been my coat of armour for lifetimes had finally cracked. The lifelong learning spree had come to end. God wanted joy for me, and so did I! Why would He want otherwise? Why should I accept anything less than joy and abundance and health and wholeness?

I dug out an old CD and slipped it into the player on my computer. God wants joy for me, I thought as I prepared my supper, barely able to stand still as the music filled the house. I had chatted with someone earlier that afternoon about joining a photography club. Pooran had tried many times to get me out of the house, to go dancing or hiking. For years, for a lifetime, for several lifetimes it seemed, my entire focus had been work, responsibilities, self-improvement, more work, more responsibilities, more self-improvement. Although I enjoyed my work, I never really did anything simply for the joy of doing it. There always had to be a reason, a need being met. Joy was a secondary benefit.

I think the day I drove out of the Kia dealership in my Soul, I brought home a lot more than a new car. Somehow, making that big financial decision for no reason other than I wanted a more enjoyable driving experience led to the crumbling of a lifetime of rigid beliefs about myself and about what life was meant to be. Life was meant to be welcomed with wonder and curiosity. Life was meant to be *lived*! God was Expressing life, beauty and harmony in every moment, every person and every thing, and I wanted to experience more of what God was Being.

God wants joy for me. I thought about this as I foxtrotted my way around the dining room table to the smooth strains of a Frank Sinatra and Tony Bennett duet. The Father was my dance partner. I laughed and I cried, overwhelmed with joy and relief. Cracked. I was cracked. No more withholding, no more limitations to the joy and the love that the Father wanted for me. No more study, analysis, searching, attempting to understand the insanity of a world of ignorance and limited perception, and, especially, no more trying to fix myself. Lifetimes of austerity barely lived in the name of spiritual pursuits came to a crashing halt. There was only Being. I did a little rumba at the far end of the dining room. Cracked. What joy! What relief!

Open House

The night before the open house, I prayed. I filled the house with love—every object, every particle, every molecule—I filled with love. God is the air that I breathe but He is also all there is. It's time to sell this house. Once more, I placed the matter in the Father's Hands, and that night, I slept peacefully, knowing that all would be well.

Five couples came to the open house. One couple came a second time with one of their fathers. And a second couple returned four times that day—the third time was to bring a verbal offer and the fourth time they actually got me out of my pyjamas to bring me the written offer. They were the perfect couple for the house. When they showed me a picture of their conure parrot named Kiwi, I knew that even the birds in the backyard would be in good company. Somehow, that made everything all right. We finalized the details of the offer that evening. They were quite eager to keep any furniture I no longer needed, and since the young man was skilled at home renovations, I was relieved of having to clear out the tool room—what I referred to as the man cave when I took visitors through the house. There was only one detail that could have caused me a little anxiety—the ten-day period they needed to update their mortgage approval.

Life Flows when Allowed

As much as I tried not to think of it, the waiting period did manage to stir up some anxiety. What if their financing was denied? I'd have to do another open house, deal with more agents and walk more strangers through the house. I really didn't have the stomach for that. Of course, when I went for my daily walks, my friend continued to help make me see things differently.

"Your good or your abundance will unfold naturally, not as a result of anything that you do. Don't base your evaluation of the truth on what you see with your eyes. Simply stand back and watch it unfold. If you interfere in any way, or if you project expectations and desires, you will cloud over the unfolding with your own limited understanding. Let that go now.

"When you step down from attempting to control life, you will find life unfolding gracefully and with ease. When you experience extreme challenge, limitations, scarcity, difficulty of any kind, it is because you have interfered with the unfolding. The more intense and effortful is your involvement in determining your own unfolding, the more challenging will be the obstacles, the more difficult and the less graceful will be unfolding.

"Your life *has* flowed with relative ease. It is because you have allowed the unfolding to occur. You have been curious and child-like in your approach. You do have the habit of working hard, which is simply a habit that needs to be relinquished because as you look back you realize that the unfolding has occurred, regardless of your effort."

It was true that when I clung to my idea of how things should unfold, I felt stress; if I clung to an idea of who should buy the house or how the sale should happen, I felt anxiety. When I stood back and watched the unfolding—when I stood way, way back without getting involved and simply did what needed to be done, monitored the sales, answered the calls, scheduled appointments for house visits—then I was not stressed and things unfolded with grace and peace. The unfolding was happening as I allowed it and it was going to happen gracefully, joyfully. In the end, I concluded that the wait was just another opportunity to deepen and strengthen my trust. Whenever my mind turned to worry, stress, anxiety or fear, I flipped the switch and went in the other direction. It was good practice.

While I was trudging through these very worldly affairs, Jesus pointed out that I was letting my so-called spirituality get in the way of the unfolding of my life. "Let it go," he said. "Life is not metaphysics or spirituality. Life is to be *lived*. Stop trying to define how it should be. Stop trying to understand it intellectually. Watch it, observe it, feel it."

It was ironic, but I had to admit that my spiritual quest had gotten in the way of my awakening.

A couple of days after I accepted the promise to purchase, I received a call from my buyers. They had obtained their financing ahead of schedule and they wanted to meet as soon as possible. Of course, I replied, feeling so completely relieved, and we fixed a date for our meeting.

"Could it be that easy?" I asked my friend the day following that meeting.

"You put it in the Hands of the Father" was his very simple answer.

Indeed, I had.

Chapter 16

All Things New

Behold, I make all things new. (Revelation, 21:5)

In mid-May, we visited the notary to transfer the deed of sale. When I woke up the following morning, I turned my thoughts to God. God is. God is Being me. God is my Source. There never had been anything for me to do. Any seeming obstacles, difficulties, pain, darkness, feelings of inadequacy or lack had all been imagined by me. Life simply unfolds. I released all thoughts of what might be and trusted that the next unfolding would occur with grace and ease. As I pondered this realization, I knew that I was loved; that *we* are loved. Tears flowed as I released any remaining need to control, letting go of my wilful desire to determine the outcome of my life, entrusting the unfolding of Me to the Father, to the Love that is our Source.

Ten days later, I picked up the keys to my new condo. That afternoon, I loaded up the car with tools, rags, toiletries and whatever might be needed to make the move as smooth as possible. A friend came along to help unload the car. As we reached the street opposite Mary's church, we gasped. In front of us was the most beautiful sunset either of us had ever seen. Just west of the condo, a sea of ruby waves washed over the sky where the sun was dropping beneath the horizon. If there was an omen of good things to come, we both agreed, this was it.

I was among the first few residents to move into the building, and the only one above the first floor. As it turned out, the builder's idea of "ready" was not quite the same as mine. The building was still a construction site. I did not have access to my parking spot in the garage because the driveway had not yet been paved; the visitor parking lot was one giant mud puddle and it was filled with dumpsters and work trucks. There were construction workers on all the floors, bricklayers climbing up the outside walls and various other tradesmen scurrying about their business. Construction debris and plaster dust covered the hallway floors, and I wouldn't have access to my balcony all summer because the railing had not been installed, which also meant that my air conditioner would not be installed. Since the garbage and recycling bins were not ready, I had to dispose of my packing materials by flinging them up into one of the dumpsters and pray they wouldn't land back on my head because it was overly full. But the elevator worked and the inside of my unit was clean. Other than lack of access to the balcony, the missing A/C and the fact that I couldn't open my windows because they were covered in protective plastic sheeting, I suppose my condo was ready.

The day after the big move, I received my brand new couch. The living room blinds had been returned to the shop due to an error in calculation, so I had leaned a couple of cardboard panels against the patio doors for a bit of privacy. Exhausted, I sat on my new couch and looked out over the panels to the open sky across the street. For the first time, I noticed the three poplars in front of my condo, their branches like arms reaching up for Heaven, high above the roofline of the building. Overnight, they had produced green leaves, the first signs of spring after a very long winter. It was windy that night, and the tall trees flowed with the westerly wind, back and forth, their long wispy forms yielding to the press of the moving air.

I decided to meditate with open eyes, and as I watched the movement of nature, I let myself flow with the poplars, leaning easily with the wind, side to side. I felt drawn to the one in the middle, sensing as though she were sent to commune with me. With each gust of wind, we leaned toward the left, toward my bedroom. I stayed in this trancelike state joined with my new friends, feeling the love and the life flowing and moving around me. I knew that I was not alone. Then the wind shifted slightly and I saw her reach out and lean further, branches opening wide, like long fingers pointing in the direction of my room. I knew she was telling me it was time to go to sleep and that I didn't need to worry and that everything would be okay. I let go, let myself feel the love and cried.

Those few weeks before and after the move were one long shopping spree. But I had adopted a new rule of shopping: get the one you like—within reason, of course. I would never be wasteful. I also honoured my body and chose organic produce whenever available, even if it was slightly more expensive. Very often, I was able to obtain those items I wanted on sale, which made the business of shopping more palatable. Other times, I was guided to an item that was more suitable. I checked in with guidance and listened as best as I could, but I still made many return trips to the stores. My name must have been on a watch list at the return counters of my favourite shopping destinations. But it didn't matter. I asked for help, listened as best I could, returned what didn't work and got the items I liked. I was learning.

While the rest of the building was moving along at a snail's pace, my condo was starting to look good. I assembled and installed countless pieces of furniture, lights, shelving, blinds, curtains and accessories. One day, when I felt I could no longer hold the screwdriver in my hand, I prayed for help, but this time, I prayed to an expert in the field, Joseph. I asked him to please help me, please give me the strength so that I could finish installing the wall shelf. Right away, I felt someone show me how to hold my elbow so I could use it as a lever when I turned the screwdriver. This position relieved the pressure from my wrist and hand, and in went the screws without a problem. What a neat trick, I thought, and I have since used this technique many times.

When I first moved in, I learned that Condo Man had left his post in the sales office. A couple of weeks later, I bumped into a lady visiting the condo across the hallway from mine. It seems that there is a place in Heaven for real estate agents after all, because they sent me one of their angels. She was newly assigned to the building, and she had to be the sweetest realtor in the universe. I forgot about all my past dealings with real estate agents, and we became fast friends.

I learned to ask for help, and also to accept help. A friend recommended a relative who was able to help with the installation of a more suitable bathroom vanity, a nicer kitchen counter and the light fixtures I preferred. Once my office was completely set up, bookcases assembled, books placed by subject, filing cabinet filled with client notes, I noticed a slightly crumpled yellow Post-it on my computer monitor. *Do you want a friend?* Of all the things to survive the mass purging and the move, I thought, and smiled. Yes, I am so very grateful for my new friends.

Without any A/C and with huge south facing windows that I couldn't open, it was hot in the condo that summer. I took three or four showers a day and some nights slept on the living room floor with my face next to the patio door. It was the coolest place in the condo. There were days when the temperature climbed into the nineties in my office. The oscillating fan I carried from room to room barely moved the hot air around. But it didn't seem to bother my clients, who just laughed it off and took it in stride. For some reason or other, those who lived in the area preferred to come in person, even though they had the option of working over Skype or the phone. With a towel on the desk next to me to mop off perspiration around my neck, I too took it in stride. Thank goodness the hot flashes were long gone!

As a mom and self-employed business owner, I was a hard-core multi-tasker. But one of the important lessons I learned during this move was to do one thing at a time. Whenever I was about to launch myself into multiple tasks, my friend reminded me, "One thing at a time." This caused me to stop a moment and centre myself. I learned that multi-tasking had been one of those ways by which the ego kept me focused on what was going on outside. By doing only one thing at a time, it is much easier to pay attention to the moment, to bless, love and be grateful for all those things that met my daily needs.

Everything in my life was new and, at times, I felt a little lost. It was as though my life was in recto verso, with everything on the opposite side from what I had been accustomed to. The old way of doing things was no longer applicable, which again caused me to stop and pay attention. All of these pauses were wonderful opportunities to stop and be curious about the true meaning of what was really there. What I saw was that, by yielding to the Father, by allowing the unfolding of my life to occur without my interference, without the need to control, with total trust, needs had been met. In fact, as I looked about the new condo and reflected on my life, it was clear that needs had always been met, in some form or other.

The condo wasn't perfect. This world will not be perfect as long as we are experiencing it incorrectly, in a way that obscures its true meaning. The perfection of the world will only be experienced when we give up our definitions and our limited way of looking. Only then will our inherent perfection be expressed and experienced in the world. But I was learning to be quiet, and look with new eyes, and from what I saw, despite its imperfections, the condo turned out to be really nice; really, really nice! And I really liked it; really, really liked it! When I looked with eyes that see truly, I could see that behind the imperfections was the perfection of God Being. Oh, and I discovered Internet radio on my Smart TV and found the perfect station: Bossa Jazz Brazil, the music of heaven, well, my heaven!

That summer I had the opportunity to work with a translator to produce a French version of *Choosing the Miracle*. This required that we go over the material together to verify that the meanings had been properly translated. I relished the thought of rereading my material about as much as I enjoyed looking at my reflection in the mirror—not very much. As we approached the end of the revision, I experienced a complete reversal of how I perceived my work. This was something I had never felt in my life, nor had it ever occurred to me that it was something I should feel. It was like I was reading the work of an unknown writer, and as I read the words of the author of that book, I felt love for her. I loved her despite the quirky wordiness and the awkward writing style; I loved her for daring to share her most intimate thoughts and feelings; I loved her for just *being* her. For the first time in my life, I loved *me*. It had never occurred to me that I could feel for "me" what I had felt for my daughters, my clients, my cat, my house or even my garden.

"Love yourself enough to take the time to *be* where you are at," my friend told me. As I burst into tears, I realized that it was not what was there that was beautiful so much as what was *not* there; it was the silence between the notes that gave meaning to all things.

There is no system, no method for awakening. There is only a willingness to allow the unfolding of Being. Each person's life, each person's script, is designed to support his or her awakening. Be where you are. It is right through the centre of your Being that the truth will be found.

Waking up was not going to be a dull or boring affair; it would not mean inactivity or withdrawal from life. I began to sense that the more I experienced peace, the more I connected with my Self, the more consistently I joined with guidance, the less defended I was about allowing the Father's Expression to be in my life, the more graceful and complete would be my unfolding. Waking up was going to mean a fuller experience with a broader awareness of the All that is going on in and around us. There is so much to live for, so much to be curious about. One thing had become clear: there would be an experience. Awakening did not mean the sudden cessation of all experiences. On the contrary, I was beginning to sense the enormity of the experience that lay in waiting once we have fully abandoned the limited experience. In truth, we wake up and Live!

This moment is new, I thought, as I walked along the main road going over the train tracks. This moment is new; it has never happened before and it will never happen again. That means that my experience of myself, the body and the world is new at each moment. All I need is to abandon my memories and my definitions and see all there is to see in the moment in all its wholeness and newness.

What is God Being now? God is Being Love. He is loving you and me while we hesitate a while. He is loving us even though we still feel the need to pursue our little dreams, knowing that nothing in Reality has been changed. Love waits for us until we decide that we want it more than we want anything else. Love waits for us because it knows that, in the end, we will choose it, because it is the substance of our Being.

Father, how still today! How quietly do all things fall in place! This is the day that has been chosen as the time in which I come to understand the lesson that there is no need that I do anything. In You is every choice already made. In You has every conflict been resolved. In You is everything I hope to find already given me. Your peace is mine. My heart is quiet, and my mind at rest. Your Love is Heaven, and Your Love is mine. (ACIM.W.286)

Epilogue

At any given moment, we are at a crossroads; no matter the circumstances in which we find ourselves, we always have only two choices.

The first choice leads to the continuation of life as we know it, perhaps with the promise of a better outcome, one day, when we have studied, learned and perfected ourselves a little bit more. We have been told that if we try hard enough, we can overcome some, perhaps even all, of our limitations and thus experience a better life. Bravely or out of fear, we stumble and fall, we cope, we engage with more dedication, we forge ahead and face what life serves up for us. Every morning we wake up and rededicate ourselves to the pursuit of our goals, to the fulfilment of our needs and our desires, in search of happiness and satisfaction. One day, we'll get there, we tell ourselves, even though the "there" of our quest seems to mysteriously morph over time.

As the years pass, we pursue this path with greater or lesser success, remaining convinced that this is all there is. We thank our fate for small mercies when things are good, and pray for mercy in times of tragedy and difficulty. Even when things go horribly wrong, every morning we get up and do it all over again, hoping that this day will bring something better. This is the path of dreaming.

The second choice does not lead to a continuation of life as we now know it. On this path, there is no success or failure; there are no needs to be met or obstacles to be overcome through hardship, sickness, suffering or pain. This path promises an experience of eternal Life, unlimited abundance, joy and wonderment. This choice leads to the true experience of Being. Above all, this path *feels* right.

Yet, this path is not chosen by many; it has a few requirements that appear difficult to meet, at least at first glance. It requires that we let go of habits and old familiar ways of seeing, as well as preconceptions, expectations, definitions and most—if not all—of our understanding of what things are or what will be.

It requires that we choose peace, for peace is the condition for this journey. We must also be open to the idea that there might very well be another way of seeing that is completely different from the way in which we have been looking at the world. This new way is made easier if we have the humility to consider that perhaps we might need a little help from someone who has already followed this path.

All that is required is the willingness to experience what Life is Being in the moment. Having set aside personal agendas, when we get up in the morning, we don garments of gratitude and wonderment; we welcome what Life will bring today. We trust implicitly that all will be well because all comes from Love. This path requires simply that we give permission for Life to be expressed. It may seem like a lot of work but, in fact, on this path, no effort is required. All that is needed is that we let go of what is not needed, all that does not belong, so that our Being can be freely expressed. This is the path of awakening. This path is beyond awesome...

Ego Flare-up Emergency Extinguishers

From *Choosing the Miracle*

Although a simple "no" will suffice when it comes to addressing an ego flare-up, being unrelenting and increasingly clever in its efforts to attract and maintain our attention, it can be helpful to have a few spare emergency responses when we feel we have lost control. Here is a list of some of my favourite ego flare-up emergency extinguishers. Feel free to add your own to this list.

- Tell yourself that God loves you, no matter what, besides which, you haven't failed because you never left home in the first place. Chances are that the ego will have a few snarky comebacks, so, move on to the next item on this list.

- Ask: Father, what is the truth here? And if that doesn't work, move on down the list.

- Forgive yourself. If you could have done it right the first time, you wouldn't be in this situation in the first place.

- Flip the switch on the ego, and move on.

- Don't analyze; you'll only be analyzing a decision made in a moment of insanity. Now, how sane is that?

- You are not the ego; the ego is no more than a bad habit.

- Remind yourself that you are the boss! The ego is a work of fiction, made up by a scared child, the part of you that is asleep.

- Be quiet and ask for help.

- Be quiet and listen for help.

- Be quiet and expect to receive help.

- Although this may be difficult at first, try peace, the ego's kryptonite.

- Don't look back; just keep moving forward.

- Find a distraction, something fun to do, something that is more important than analyzing your screw-up.

- The ego analyzes; the Holy Spirit accepts.

- Remind yourself that your brother/sister is just like you, afraid of love.
- I am never upset for the reason I think.
- The ego always lies; don't even bother trying to reason with it.
- Don't ruminate, cogitate or try to understand why you messed up. You left your wholeness for a moment because you were afraid of love. Period.
- Your brother/sister is calling for love. If that doesn't motivate you to choose peace, see next point.
- We go home together, or not at all. Awakening is a two-person job.
- Choosing the miracle is a habit. It undoes the bad habit of choosing to believe the ego's lies.
- In case you missed it, just keep moving forward!
- Go for a walk, listen to music, have a cookie or two or three.
- Call a friend or family member and talk about something that concerns them.
- Do not bring this up for analysis with your therapist, don't text it to your BFF. The point is to deflate it, and the only way to do that is to not give it any attention.
- The ego thrives and survives on the attention you give it.
- Remind yourself that your real job is to be the light for your brothers and sisters. Do it for them.
- Treat yourself, your brothers and sisters, every object, animate or inanimate, with dignity and respect, for all there is before you is God and His creation.
- If none of this works, enjoy the ego flare-up, wallow in it, bask in it, but don't feel guilty about it. Then, try to recall what it feels like to be at peace. Peace probably feels much better than an ego flare-up. Next time, you'll choose differently.
- God loves you.
- Now, move forward.

Bibliography

All references to *A Course in Miracles* are from the Sparkly Edition. Available for download or purchase Online at http://acimsearch.org/get-a-sparkly/. Text (T), Workbook (W), Manual (M)

Bible quotes are from the New King James Version.

Quote from *The Song of Prayer* is from *A Course in Miracles*, the Combined Volume, Third Edition, 2007. Published by the Foundation for Inner Peace, P.O. Box 598, Mill Valley, CA 94942.

Edward, Pauline. *Choosing the Miracle*. Montreal, Canada: Desert Lily Publications, 2012.

Tuttle, Paul Norman. *Graduation: The End of Illusions*. The Northwest Foundation for *A Course in Miracles*,1991.

————. *You are the Answer: A Journey of Awakening*. The Northwest Foundation for *A Course in Miracles*, 1985.

INTERNET RESOURCES

Please visit the author's website for links,
book reviews and additional resources.
www.PaulineEdward.com

Choosing the Miracle
Pauline Edward
Desert Lily Publications, Montreal, Canada

This book was nearly three quarters of the way finished when, seven years into her work with *A Course in Miracles*, the author hit a wall. Although it appeared as a very high wall that would take a very long time and a whole lot of effort to be climbed, as it turned out, it simply needed to be risen above and left behind. This passing hurdle resulted in the crumbling of a lifetime of learning and a major shift in perception, the ideal condition for a true experience of the miracle. Written with the same candour, sincerity, wit and courage, this book picks up where *Leaving the Desert* left off and will be an inspiration for all spiritual seekers.

"The greatest compliment an author of a spiritual book can receive is that their extension of love is felt throughout the book. I found that *Choosing the Miracle* not only inspired me, but gave me a direct experience of God."
—Reverend Dan Costello

"In *Choosing the Miracle*, Pauline Edward graciously plants yet another shimmering guidepost for her fellow Course students. By sharing the entertaining insights gleaned from her own ongoing growth with *A Course in Miracles*, Pauline Edward looks through the ceaseless lies of the ego to reveal the truth of spirit. Stay on Course by *Choosing the Miracle*."
—Alexander Marchand, author of *The Universe Is a Dream*

"*Choosing the Miracle* is a wonderful read for any serious student of *A Course in Miracles*. It reveals the true simplicity of the Course's message, and offers insight for applying the Course into our every day lives and every encounter. Moments of realization are ours to experience when we simply make the choice. And when we join Pauline Edward on her journey in *Choosing the Miracle* we witness the true simplicity in making the choice... the true simplicity of living the "Miracle.""

"In *Choosing the Miracle* Pauline Edward not only shows us the simplicity of living *A Course in Miracles*, she shares with us, through her personal journey, how our Truth is right here, right now. No more waiting, no more searching. Enlightenment is not only for a select few. It is not out of our reach. It is for everyone, right here, right now!

"If you've read *A Course in Miracles* over, maybe completed the Workbook lessons more than once and you are done with baby steps and are now hungry to witness the Truth every day of your life, then I recommend reading Pauline Edward's book *Choosing the Miracle*. The message is powerful. Heaven is right here, right now. Why wait a minute longer? When you can be CHOOSING the MIRACLE today!

"*Choosing the Miracle* is a wonderful account of the simplicity of actually "living" *A Course in Miracles*, and opens the door for dedicated students who are WILLING to live and walk the Truth right here, right now, TODAY!"

—Robyn Busfield, Author of *Forgiveness Is the Home of Miracles*

Leaving the Desert
Embracing the Simplicity of *A Course in Miracles*
Pauline Edward
Desert Lily Publications, Montreal, Canada

After completing a first reading of *A Course in Miracles*, the most challenging read of her life, the author exclaimed, "Never again!" Yet, she knew that if she were to make real progress with her lifelong spiritual quest, she would need a thorough understanding of the Course's unique thought system. So, back to school she went—the school of life, that is. Though a seasoned seeker, never did she anticipate the dark nights she would encounter along the journey, nor the gift of grace that would pull her through. Readers will delight in the same profound spiritual insight, candour, humour and lively writing style as found in *Making Peace with God*.

"*Leaving the Desert: Embracing the Simplicity of A Course in Miracles*, is one of the most practical spiritual books ever written. I was struck by Pauline's ability to clearly and simply state the principles of the Course, from the beginning of her journey, through a genuine spiritual search, to her discovery of a new direction, to the understanding of miracles, and ultimately to the miracle of forgiveness in undoing the deviousness of the ego. I highly recommend this book to anyone who is on a spiritual path, and especially to those who want to get on the fast track."
—Gary Renard, Best-selling author of *The Disappearance of the Universe*

"I thoroughly enjoyed *Leaving the Desert* by Pauline Edward. It is an excellent description of the basic metaphysics and psychology of *A Course in Miracles* and its practical application in daily life, written in a clear conversational style."
—Jon Mundy, Ph.D., author of *Living A Course in Miracles*

"In *Leaving the Desert: Embracing the Simplicity of A Course in Miracles*, Pauline Edward shares her intimate quest both to fully comprehend the Course's fundamental principles despite the ego's

formidable resistance and to apply its unique forgiveness in her daily life. *Leaving the Desert* will inspire Course newbies and veterans alike with its profound, comprehensive understanding and specific examples fearlessly and generously drawn from the classroom of the author's life."
—Susan Dugan, author of *Extraordinary Ordinary Forgiveness*

"Written with humor and courageous self-disclosure, Pauline Edward's *Leaving the Desert* is a delight. Through sharing her own exploration—her commitment and her doubts—she addresses all the major topics covered in *A Course in Miracles* with precision and clarity. For new students as well as veterans of the Course, her overview of its purpose and methodology is excellent. Her adroit sprinkling of personal anecdotes enlivens and clarifies her path (and ours) and her honesty allows the book to be a comforting companion to those seeking to engage more artfully with this life-changing practice. You will read this book with a smile of recognition and gratitude."
—Carol Howe, author of *Never Forget to Laugh: Personal Recollections of Bill Thetford, Co-scribe of A COURSE IN MIRACLES*

"Pauline Edward delivers the concepts of *A Course in Miracles* elegantly and uncompromisingly, and with an undeniably gifted style. This book is wonderful. It offers a deep and much-needed exploration of the core message of *A Course in Miracles*. It comes from profound guidance, and places the reader at the altar of Truth. *Leaving the Desert* is a must-read for any student of the Course, or any person seeking enlightenment, who would leave no stone unturned in an endeavour to return Home to our natural state of Love."
—Robyn Busfield, author of *Forgiveness Is the Home of Miracles*

Making Peace with God
The Journey of a *Course in Miracles* Student
Pauline Edward
Desert Lily Publications, Montreal, Canada

It is said, "Seek and you will find." But what happens when your quest for the truth about life, God and the meaning of existence repeatedly fails to offer satisfactory answers? Determined to uncover the truth, you persist, and, lo and behold, you find. But what if the truth you discover challenges each and every one of your beliefs? This is the story of one woman's lifelong search for a fulfilling spirituality, one that answers the unanswerable, that is truly universal and all-inclusive and, above all, that is logical and practicable. *Making Peace with God* recounts a journey that begins with Roman Catholicism, explores various ancient and contemporary spiritualities and culminates with the extraordinary thought system of *A Course in Miracles*.

Gary Renard, best-selling author of *The Disappearance of the Universe* highly recommends this wonderful book.

"A must read for *A Course in Miracles* students or anyone curious about its profound, mind-healing message."
—Susan Dugan, author of *Extraordinary Ordinary Forgiveness*

"*Making Peace with God* is the ultimate destination of all spiritual journeys... a story sure to save much time for the spiritual seeker."
—Alexander Marchand, author and artist of *The Universe Is a Dream: The Secrets of Existence Revealed*

"An inspiring and enjoyable book which will encourage others on their spiritual journey."
—Michael Dawson, author of *Healing the Cause*

"I recommend *Making Peace with God* to anyone who would like good company on the path!"
—Jennifer Hadley

The Power of Time
Understanding the Cycles of Your Life's Path
Pauline Edward
Llewellyn Worldwide, Ltd. Woodbury, MN

Don't wait around for life to just "happen." Develop a solid, successful life plan with guidance from astrologer-numerologist Pauline Edward. Whether your goals are personal or professional, *The Power of Time* will help you take advantage of the powerful natural cycles at work in your life. Simple calculations based on numerology reveal where you are in each nine-year cycle and what to expect from each year, month and day. With your life path clearly mapped out, it will be easy for you to pinpoint the best times to start a new job, focus on family, launch a business, take time to reflect, make a major purchase, complete a project, expand your horizons and more.

"I've used numerology for nearly 30 years. This tool is accurate, exciting, and helpful. *The Power of Time* will show you how."
—Christiane Northrup, MD, author of *Women's Bodies, Women's Wisdom* and *The Wisdom of Menopause*

"A top-notch reference, one that will excite and instruct anyone about the power of numbers in your life."
—*Dell Horoscope*

"This immensely readable book is a fascinating introduction to the subject of numerology. Best of all, *The Power of Time* takes the reader by the hand and shows her how to apply the concepts to her own life. I found the workbook sections especially helpful and could not put the book down until I had charted my own Life Path Number, Personal Year Number and 9-Year Epicycle. *The Power of Time* is a unique and insightful contribution to the many books available on setting goals and making short- and long-term career plans."
—CJ Carmichael, best-selling romance author

Astrological Crosses
Exploring the Cardinal, Fixed and Mutable Modes
Pauline Edward
Desert Lily Publications, Montreal, Canada

For the first time ever, here is an astrology book that focuses on astrological crosses (the cardinal, fixed and mutable aspects of the signs of the zodiac) and their impact on people's lives, behaviour, actions and motivation. Crosses are so important to truly understanding a chart that you will wonder how you ever completed an astrological analysis without this essential component. *Astrological Crosses in Relationships* explores the strengths and challenges of each cross, using many real-life stories taken from the author's consulting practice. With this innovative guide, you can learn to identify crosses in everyday life experiences, mend star-crossed relationships and balance a lack or overemphasis of crosses in your birth chart.

"Pauline Edward's book helps us understand why people think and communicate the way they do, which in turn helps us to improve our relationships. That's no small feat! In-depth, well-written, and informative… A valuable asset to anyone interested in understanding human behaviour."
—Lucy MacDonald, MEd, author of *Learn to Be an Optimist*

"The best book yet about the nature of cardinal, fixed, and mutable. Her readable, insightful work can help both beginning and experienced astrologers gain much understanding about life's processes. Highly recommended."
—Michael Munkasey, PMAFA, NCGR-IV

"Absolutely excellent work on the cardinal, fixed and mutable qualities of the signs. Suitable for any level of astrologer, this goes into the subject at a deeper level than I've seen before. Thought-provoking and intelligently written."
—*The Wessex Astrologer*

About the Author

Pauline Edward is an astrologer-numerologist, speaker and Certified Professional Coach and Group Leader. She is the founder of A Time for Success, a consulting business specializing in Trends, Cycles and Lifestyle Planning, offering consultations and workshops for individuals and businesses worldwide. She is the recipient of a Chamber of Commerce Accolades Award for excellence in business practice.

With a background in the sciences and a fascination for all things mystical, Pauline's journey has been enriched by a wide range of experiences from research in international economics, technical writing in R & D and computer training, to studies in astrology, numerology, meditation, yoga, shamanism, the Bach Flower Remedies, herbology, healing and reiki. Her lifelong quest for truth and an understanding of the meaning of life eventually led her to *A Course in Miracles*, a teaching that has now become an integral part of her life.

Pauline is available for consultations, coaching, speaking engagements and workshops. For information about services, upcoming events and publications, visit her website: www.paulineedward.com

CPSIA information can be obtained at www.ICGtesting.com
Printed in the USA
BVOW02s2004130814

362729BV00010B/613/P

9 780986 890963